The

FRUITFUL
LIFE

The FRUITFUL LIFE

THE OVERFLOW
of GOD'S LOVE THROUGH YOU

JERRY BRIDGES

NAVPRESS

Discipleship Inside Out™

NavPress is the publishing ministry of The Navigators, an international Christian organization and leader in personal spiritual development. NavPress is committed to helping people grow spiritually and enjoy lives of meaning and hope through personal and group resources that are biblically rooted, culturally relevant, and highly practical.

**For a free catalog go to www.NavPress.com
or call 1.800.366.7788 in the United States or 1.800.839.4769 in Canada.**

www.navpress.com

NAVPRESS and the NAVPRESS logo are registered trademarks of NavPress. Absence of ® in connection with marks of NavPress or other parties does not indicate an absence of registration of those marks.

ISBN-13: 978-1-60006-027-4

Cover design by Studiogearbox.com
Cover photo by Jerry Driendl/Getty
Creative Team: Don Simpson, Karen Lee-Thorp, Cara Iverson, Arvid Wallen, Bob Bubnis, Kathy Guist

This book incorporates content originally included in *The Practice of Godliness*, copyright © 1983, 2004 by Jerry Bridges and published by NavPress.

Some of the anecdotal illustrations in this book are true to life and are included with the permission of the persons involved. All other illustrations are composites of real situations, and any resemblance to people living or dead is coincidental.

Unless otherwise identified, all Scripture quotations in this publication are taken from the HOLY BIBLE: NEW INTERNATIONAL VERSION® (NIV®). Copyright © 1973, 1978, 1984 by International Bible Society. Used by permission of Zondervan Publishing House. All rights reserved. Other versions used include: the *New American Standard Bible* (NASB), © The Lockman Foundation 1960, 1962, 1963, 1968, 1971, 1972, 1973, 1975, 1977, 1995; the *Amplified New Testament* (AMP), © The Lockman Foundation 1954, 1958; the *English Standard Version* (ESV), copyright © 2001 by Crossway Bibles, a division of Good News Publishers. Used by permission. All rights reserved; the *Good News Bible Today's English Version* (TEV), copyright © American Bible Society 1966, 1971, 1976; and the *King James Version* (KJV).

Bridges, Jerry.
    The fruitful life : the overflow of God's love through you / Jerry Bridges.
    p. cm.
    Includes bibliographical references.
    ISBN 1-60006-027-7
    1. Christian life. 2. Fruit of the Spirit. I. Title.
BV4501.3.B748 2006   241'.4--dc22
                                    2006019676
                                      CIP

Printed in the United States of America

7 8 9 10 11 / 14 13 12 11

Contents

Preface
7

1. Taking On God's Character
Ephesians 4:22-24
11

2. Devotion to God
Revelation 15:4
29

3. Humility
Luke 18:14
47

4. Love
Colossians 3:14
61

5. Joy
Romans 14:17
75

6. Peace
Romans 12:18
89

7. Patience
Colossians 3:12-13
103

8. Kindness and Goodness
Galatians 6:10
117

9. Faithfulness
Proverbs 20:6
129

10. Gentleness
Galatians 5:22-23 / Colossians 3:12
141

11. Self-Control
Proverbs 25:28
153

12. Seeking a Deeper Devotion
Psalm 119:10
169

Notes
181

Author
187

Preface

Healthy human life is fruitful life. We sense this at a deep level. For instance, the desire for abundance can bring forth a home with children, a bountiful flower garden, a farm flourishing with crops, a job with creative opportunities, a business with steady growth, an expanding role in public leadership, or simply the sharing of wisdom with others.

The model for fruitfulness is God. He created the universe in a magnificent display of His extravagance, then turned to His living creatures and said, "Be fruitful and multiply" (Genesis 1:28, NASB). There is a generational fruitfulness—both biological and spiritual—intended and prompted by God. But there is also a fruitfulness through the traits of Christian character. Professor John Murray wrote, "Whatever else we may have, if we do not have character we have nothing. It is character that determines destiny."[1]

Christian character arises from "participation in the divine nature" (2 Peter 1:4) and is the work of the Holy Spirit. This book is about the fruit of the Spirit—the nine character qualities found in Galatians 5:22-23: love, joy, peace, patience, kindness, goodness, faithfulness, gentleness, and self-control. In my 1983 book titled *The Practice of Godliness*, I presented much of the content of this present book. In that previous work, I examined a number of qualities that I identified as traits of godly character, which include these nine traits in Galatians 5:22-23.

Recently, I have felt the need to revisit discussion of the fruit of the Spirit as a specific focus. Since writing *The Practice of Godliness*, much has changed in the spiritual landscape of the evangelical church. For one thing, "spiritual formation" has become an area of rising interest and practice in seminaries, among church leaders, and in the lives of thousands of laypeople.

This is a praiseworthy movement among evangelicals for which we can be truly grateful to God. As it proceeds, however, it will be important for the movement to head in the right direction. I agree with Evan Howard that "Christian spiritual formation is not simply fostering the *experience* of the Spirit but rather a radical *formation*, a shaping and molding of the believer into conformity with Christ through the Spirit."[2] In other words, spiritual formation must shape character in keeping with the classic, biblical understanding of godliness.

We should also notice that the fruit of the Spirit is both formational and *relational*—not just a matter for private experience. For example, "joy" is most accurately "joy in the Holy Spirit" (Romans 14:17), "peace" is the peace Christ gives us (see John 14:27), and "love comes from God" (1 John 4:7). Further, several of these character qualities have a definite outward focus toward other people. They require practice in the midst of the world. As Jonathan Edwards said, "All true Christian grace tends to holy practice."[3]

Another reason for revisiting the fruit of the Spirit is that I often hear a certain possessiveness today about "my spiritual gifts." Certainly, we can be thankful that in the last generation there has been a thriving literature on spiritual gifts. But again, sometimes there is a self-focus for the gifts. We use "assessment instruments" to nail down what our gifts are and seek to use them in a way that can tend toward personal fulfillment. The danger is that the gifts of the Spirit will be separated from the fruit of the Spirit. This can lead to prideful ambition rather than humble, loving service. Sinclair B. Ferguson writes that the fruit of the Spirit "should be distinguished from the gifts of the Spirit, but ought never to be absent in their exercise. For without love, and the humility which accompanies it . . . the purpose of the gifts of the Spirit is thwarted."[4]

The Puritan writer John Owen vigorously insisted that the fruit of the Spirit is the work of the Spirit and not of human origin.[5] These godly qualities are not something we can manufacture, take pride in, or lay claim to as self-generated. Rather, they are the work of God, and their source is God alone. However, we have a crucial role to play. I call these character traits "garments of grace" because we must actively put them on. As Owen explained, we are responsible for acts of obedience by which this fruit is "preserved, increased, strengthened, and improved."[6]

With these thoughts in mind, I offer the following study on the fruit of the Spirit, which includes exercises at the end of each chapter. "Love is no ingredient in a merely speculative faith," Jonathan Edwards noted, "but it is the life and soul of a practical faith."[7]

Before we look at the fruit of the Spirit, we will first examine how these traits are cultivated through devotion to God in Christ, the true Vine from which this abundant fruit overflows through us.

Taking On God's Character

You were taught, with regard to your former way of life, to put off your old self, which is being corrupted by its deceitful desires; to be made new in the attitude of your minds; and to put on the new self, created to be like God in true righteousness and holiness.

EPHESIANS 4:22-24

Fruitful character comes from a great devotion, and the greatest devotion of all is the love of God. A life that grows in loving God becomes like God. John Owen writes, "[Love] begets a likeness between the mind loving and the object beloved. . . . A mind filled with the love of Christ as crucified . . . will be changed into his image and likeness."[1] The apostle Paul writes,

> And we all, with unveiled face, beholding the glory of the Lord, are being transformed into the same image from one degree of glory to another. For this comes from the Lord who is the Spirit. (2 Corinthians 3:18, ESV)

Christian character flows out of devotion to God, and it confirms the reality of that devotion in practical ways. We may express a reverence for God, we may lift our hearts in worship to Him, but we demonstrate the genuineness of our devotion to God by our earnest desire and sincere effort to be like Him. Paul not only wanted to know Christ, he wanted to be like Him, and he pressed forward with utmost intensity toward that goal.

In the Scripture text that opened this chapter, Paul says we must "put on the new self" and "be made new in the attitude of your minds." What is this new attitude of mind, and where does it come from? Again, John Owen helps us here. He writes that this is the "image of God" and "the divine nature" that is wrought in us by God and that we partake of by the Spirit of God. It is a "supernatural habit" or a "habit of grace" that is "nothing but the word changed into grace in our hearts."[2]

What are the character traits that distinguish the person who is increasing in this habit of grace — the person who is becoming godlike? A good place to start is the list of nine gracious qualities, which Paul calls the fruit of the Spirit, in Galatians 5:22-23. In chapters to come, we will concentrate on these qualities. It seems obvious, however, that Paul did not intend to limit the traits of the Spirit's fruit just to this well-known list. Any other trait commended in Scripture as befitting a believer is also a fruit of the Spirit, since its evidence is a result only of the Spirit's ministry in our hearts. To the qualities listed in Galatians 5 — love, joy, peace, patience, kindness, goodness, faithfulness, gentleness, and self-control — we can also add such traits as holiness, humility, compassion, forbearance, contentment, thankfulness, considerateness, sincerity, and perseverance.[3] We devote a whole chapter of this book (chapter 3) to humility because it is so foundational to the other traits.

This is an awesome list of character traits to pursue, and our first reaction, if we are realistic at all, is probably to say, "I can't work on all of these." That is indeed true, *if* we were left to our own devices. But these traits are the fruit of the Spirit, the result of *His* work within us. This means not that we bear no responsibility for the development of Christian character but rather that we fulfill our responsibility under His direction and by His enablement. It is this divine dimension that makes Christian character possible, and it is only this divine dimension that can keep us from becoming frustrated and defeated in our desire to exemplify godly character traits in our lives.

Each of chapters 4 to 11 focus on one of the nine traits Paul calls "the fruit of the Spirit." There are some basic principles, however, that apply to all aspects of godly character.

THE RIGHT MOTIVE

The first principle of the "habit of grace" (or what I will often call "godliness," "godlikeness," or "Christlikeness" in this book) is, *Devotion to God is the only acceptable motive for actions that are pleasing to God.* This devotion may express itself in one of several different ways. We may have a sincere desire to please God or to glorify Him; we may do or not do a particular action because we love God or because we sense that He is worthy of our obedience. However our motivation expresses itself, if it is God-centered, it arises out of our devotion to God and is acceptable to Him.

Unfortunately, too often our motives are self-centered rather than God-centered. We want to maintain our reputation before others, or we want to feel good about ourselves. Or we may even seek to live a decent and moral life or to do good deeds because such an ethic has been instilled in us from childhood. But that motivation is never related to God and thus is not acceptable to Him.

When Joseph was enticed by Potiphar's wife, he did not refuse her on the basis, "If I did that and my master found out, he would have my head." No, he said, "How then could I do such a wicked thing and sin against God?" (Genesis 39:9). His motivation for morality was centered in God, and because of that it was acceptable to God.

I recall once being tempted with the opportunity to engage in a questionable business transaction, one of those gray-area situations in which we tend to rationalize our actions. As I pondered the matter, I thought, *I better not; I might incur the discipline of God.* Now, when all proper motives fail, it is certainly better to be checked by the fear of God's discipline than to go ahead with our sin. But that is not the right motive. In this situation, the Holy Spirit came to my aid, and I thought to myself, *I realize that the fear of God's discipline is certainly an unworthy motive, but the real reason I should not do that is because God is worthy of my most honorable conduct.* The Holy Spirit helped me recognize the self-centeredness of my initial motivation and correctly focus my motivation on God.

When God commanded Abraham to offer up Isaac as a sacrifice, He tested his motive. As He stayed Abraham's knife from the fatal plunge, God said, "Now I know that you fear God, because you have not withheld from me your son, your only son" (Genesis 22:12). It was Abraham's fear of God that motivated him to go forward with that supreme act of obedience. We usually associate Abraham's obedience with his faith. It was by faith that Abraham was *enabled* to offer Isaac as a sacrifice, but it was the fear of God that *motivated* him. And it was this godward motivation that the Lord saw and accepted and commended.

As we look into the New Testament, we see this godward motivation emphasized again and again. Jesus taught that all the Law and the Prophets hang on the two commandments of love for God and love for our neighbor (see Matthew 22:37-40). He was teaching not merely that these two commandments of love sum up all the other more specific commandments but rather that all the other commandments depend upon the motivation of love for their fulfillment. The fear of consequences may keep us from committing the outward acts of murder or adultery, but only love will keep us from committing murder or adultery in our hearts.

In 1 Corinthians 10:31, Paul tells us that even our eating and drinking is to be done for the glory of God. As someone has observed, there is nothing more ordinary and routine than our eating and drinking; yet even this is to be done with a godward motivation. Slaves were enjoined to obey their earthly masters out of "reverence for the Lord" (Colossians 3:22). All of us are to submit ourselves to human authority "for the Lord's sake" (1 Peter 2:13). And our interpersonal relationships — our mutual submission to one another — is to be done "out of reverence for Christ" (Ephesians 5:21). All of our actions, to be acceptable to God, must be done out of a sense of devotion to God.

THE SOURCE OF POWER

The second principle of godly character is, *The power or enablement for a godly life comes from the risen Christ.* Paul says in relation to his ministry, "Our competence comes from God" (2 Corinthians 3:5), and "I labor, struggling with all his energy, which so powerfully works in me" (Colossians 1:29). He says of his ability to be content in any situation, "I can do everything through him who gives me strength" (Philippians 4:13).

It is very likely that God, in His sovereign calling and preparation of Paul for his tremendous task, had endowed him with more noble qualities and strength of character than any person since; yet Paul consistently attributes his spiritual strength and accomplishments to the Lord's power. I once heard someone say, "When I do something wrong, I have to take the blame, but when I do something right, God gets the credit." This person was complaining, but he was exactly correct. Certainly, God cannot be blamed for our sins, but only He can provide the spiritual power to enable us to live godly lives.

As the *source* of power for Christlike character is Christ, so the *means* of experiencing that power is through our relationship with Him. This truth is Jesus' essential teaching in His illustration in John 15 of the vine and the branches. It is only by abiding in Him that we can bring forth the fruit of godly character.[4] The most helpful explanation I have found of what it means to abide in Christ comes from the nineteenth-century Swiss theologian Frederic Louis Godet: "'To abide in me' expresses the continual act by which the Christian sets aside everything which he might derive from his own wisdom, strength, merit, to draw all from Christ."[5]

Paul expresses this relationship as "living in Christ." He says in Colossians 2:6-7, "So then, just as you received Christ Jesus as Lord, continue to live in him, rooted and built up in him, strengthened in the faith." The context of this statement is that all the wisdom and power for living the Christian life are to be found in Christ rather than in man-made philosophies and moralisms (see verses 2-4,8-10). This is what Godet is saying. We have to set aside any dependence upon our own wisdom and strength of character and draw all that we need from Christ through faith in Him. This faith, of course, is expressed concretely by prayer to Him. Psalm 119:33-37 is a good example of such a prayer of dependence.

This relationship is also maintained by beholding the glory of Christ in His Word. As we learned on page 11, in 2 Corinthians 3:18, Paul tells us that as we behold the Lord's glory, we are transformed more and more into His image. Beholding the Lord's glory in His Word is more than observing His humanity in the Gospels; it is observing His character, His attributes, and His will in every page of Scripture. And as we observe Him, as we maintain this relationship with Him through His Word, we are transformed more and more into His likeness; we are enabled by the Holy Spirit to progressively manifest the graces of godly character.

So it is this relationship with Christ, expressed by beholding Him in His Word and depending upon Him in prayer, that enables us to draw from Him the power essential for a Christlike life. The Christian is not like an automobile with a self-contained power source; rather, he is like an electric motor that must be constantly connected to an outside current for its power. Our source of power is in the risen Christ, and we stay connected to Him by beholding Him in His Word and depending on Him in prayer.

RESPONSIBILITY AND DEPENDENCE

The third principle of godly character is, *Though the power for Christlike character comes from Christ, the responsibility for developing and displaying that character is ours.* This principle seems to be one of the most difficult for us to understand and apply. One day we sense our personal responsibility and seek to live a godly life by the strength of our own willpower. The next day, realizing the futility of trusting in ourselves, we turn it all over to Christ and abdicate our responsibility, which is set forth in the Scriptures. We need to learn that the Bible teaches both total responsibility and total dependence in all aspects of the Christian life.

I once read a statement to the effect that there is nothing a Christian can do to develop the fruit of the Spirit in his life; it is all the work of the Holy Spirit. Sensing that at best such a statement failed to present a balance of scriptural truth, I took out my concordance and looked up various passages that referred to one or more of the nine character traits listed as fruit of the Spirit in Galatians 5. For every one of those traits, I found one or more passages in which we are commanded to exhibit them. We are enjoined to love, to rejoice, to live in peace with each other, and so forth. These commands address our responsibility.

When Paul describes his own pursuit of a godlike life, he uses strong verbs such as "press on" and "straining toward" (Philippians 3:12-14). These words convey the idea of intense effort on his part and communicate forcefully his own sense of personal responsibility. He tells Timothy, "Train yourself to be godly" (1 Timothy 4:7). The Greek word rendered "train" here originally referred to the training of athletes.

The solution to the seemingly incompatible statements that we are both totally responsible and totally dependent is found in Philippians 2:12-13:

> Therefore, my dear friends, as you have always obeyed — not only in my presence, but now much more in my absence — continue to work out your salvation with fear and trembling, for it is God who works in you to will and to act according to his good purpose.

Commenting on this passage, Professor Jac J. Müller says, "The believer is called to self-activity, to the active pursuit of the will of God, to the promotion of the spiritual life in himself, to the realization of the virtues of the Christian life, and to a personal application of salvation."[6] If we stopped at this point, it would appear that we are left to our own devices, to our own strength of character and our own willpower. But Paul does not stop with our responsibility. He says, "For it is God who works in you." The spiritual power that enables us to apply ourselves to the cultivation of Christian graces is of God, who works in us to will and to act.

Nineteenth-century Dutch Reformed pastor George W. Bethune puts it this way:

> While, therefore, we grow in the Christian life by divine grace, it is *our duty* to grow in grace. Besides, the quality

of grace is such that, though it is strength from God, we must use it. Grace gives no new faculty, but strengthens the faculties which we have. . . . Hence the fruits of the Spirit are the qualities and actions of the renewed man, not produced without him, but wrought through him. . . . Let us then be ever mindful of our entire dependence upon the Spirit of God . . . [but] let us be ever mindful of our duty "to maintain good works."[7]

PUT OFF AND PUT ON

The fourth principle of godly character is, *The development of godly character entails both putting off and putting on character traits.* As we saw at the beginning of this chapter, Paul says,

> You were taught, with regard to your former way of life, to put off your old self, which is being corrupted by its deceitful desires; to be made new in the attitude of your minds; and to *put on the new self*, created to be like God in true righteousness and holiness. (Ephesians 4:22-24, emphasis added)

In the succeeding verses (4:25–5:4), Paul makes some very specific applications of this principle. We are to put off falsehood and put on truthfulness. We are to put off stealing and put on generosity. Unwholesome talk must be put off and replaced with speech that is helpful for building others up. Bitterness, rage, anger, and slander are to be replaced with kindness, compassion, and forgiveness. Obscene or suggestive speech is to be replaced with thanksgiving. Even Paul's list of gracious qualities in Galatians 5, called the fruit of the Spirit, is set in contrast to a lengthy catalog of vices of the sinful nature that the godly person must put off.

It was said of the Lord Jesus that He both loved righteousness and hated wickedness (see Hebrews 1:9). And we are to follow His example, for Paul instructs us to "hate what is evil; cling to what is good" (Romans 12:9). Surely we must put to death, by the aid of the Holy Spirit, the misdeeds of the body. But we must also, again with His enablement, clothe ourselves with compassion, kindness, humility, gentleness, and patience.

Just as we need to learn Scripture's teaching for the dual principle of personal responsibility and total dependence, here also we need to seek the balance of Scripture in putting off and putting on. Some Christians have a tendency to emphasize only putting off traits of the sinful nature. They are usually very morally upright but lacking in those gracious qualities of love, joy, and compassion. When a fellow Christian falls into sin, they seek not to restore the erring one gently but rather to ostracize him or her from their fellowship. A repentant Christian once wrote me that his church knew how to reach out to lost sinners but did not know how to restore one of its own errant members. This is the attitude we tend to develop when we put our entire emphasis in Christian character growth on putting off sinful habits.

But there is equal danger if we focus all our attention on such qualities as love and compassion while neglecting to deal with the vices of the sinful nature. Today there is a good deal of emphasis on affirming and encouraging one another. We are to help one another "feel good about ourselves." We undoubtedly need such encouragement in the body of Christ, but we must not neglect the equally scriptural emphasis of putting to death the deeds of the sinful nature.

We are to put off the traits of the old self and put on the traits of the new. If we desire to be godly, we must not neglect either of these biblical emphases.

BALANCED GROWTH

The fifth principle of godly character is, *We are to pursue growth in all of the graces that are considered the fruit of the Spirit.* This would include traits such as compassion, forbearance, and humility that are not included in the nine-trait list of Galatians 5 but are obviously a result of His ministry in our lives. Godly character is balanced. It displays with equal emphasis the entire spectrum of graces that are set forth in the Scriptures as characteristic of the godly person.

We tend to emphasize in our lives those traits that seem most natural to our particular temperaments. But the fruit of the Spirit is not a matter of temperament; it is the result of the individual Christian seeking to grow, under the direction and aid of the Spirit, in every area of Christian character. Though in this book we will examine primarily the nine traits listed in Galatians 5, we should keep in mind a lifelong objective of growing in all the traits of godliness.

If we have an outgoing and buoyant personality, we often respond easily to the admonition to rejoice in the Lord or to be compassionate and tenderhearted. At the same time, we may find it difficult to exercise self-control or be faithful with responsibilities. Our personality type must pray more earnestly and strive more diligently for these latter graces. Above all, we must be convinced of the necessity of those graces that are most difficult to display. We must not excuse ourselves for our lack of faithfulness on the basis of, "That's just the way I am."

Similarly, if we are even-tempered and unemotional, we may easily respond to the need for faithfulness but may have difficulty with the fruit of joy. I personally identify with this type of personality. Faithfulness is very high in my value system; when given a responsibility, I am usually conscientious about fulfilling it. But I have to give special attention to joy. A number of years ago, God brought to my attention that "the kingdom of God is not a matter of eating and drinking, but of righteousness, peace and joy in the Holy Spirit" (Romans 14:17). I realized that joy in the Lord was just as important as any other trait of godly character. (We will look more closely at joy in chapter 5.)

Furthermore, even those traits to which we most naturally respond need to be developed under the ministry of the Spirit. God has a way of putting us in situations that exercise our character in those areas where we feel we are strong, so that the fruit might be of the Spirit, not of ourselves. For example, the naturally faithful person might stop short of dependability if it becomes inconvenient, but the godly person keeps his or her word even when it is costly.

If our personality is such that self-discipline comes easily to us, we may not understand why anyone else has difficulty with self-control. We may be so self-disciplined that this trait of godly character seems to come quite naturally. But as a godly person seeking to display all the fruit of the Spirit, we may weep over our lack of patience and gentleness in our relationships with others.

If we are melancholy in personality, we may be sensitive to the needs of others and often self-sacrificing in our relationships. At the same time, we may have a tendency to be critical and unforgiving, so we need to especially look to the Holy Spirit for our ministry in those areas of need.

· I do not intend this section to be an amateur psychological analysis of various temperament types. Rather, I am seeking to demonstrate the varying needs each of us will have in displaying the fruit of the Spirit in our lives. The principle to learn and apply is, *We are responsible for exhibiting all of the traits of godly character in a balanced fashion.* Some traits are more difficult to grow in than others. These will require extra prayer and attention on our part, but that is simply the price we must pay to grow in godlikeness.

GROWTH IS PROGRESSIVE

The sixth principle of godly character is, *Growth in all areas is progressive and never finished.* Even the apostle Paul recognized this truth in his own life. In the context of his great longing to know Christ and be like Him, he said, "Not that I have already obtained all this, or have already been made perfect, but I press on" (Philippians 3:12). In prison, near the end of his apostolic career, he was still pressing on, exerting every effort to continue growing in his knowledge and likeness of Christ.

Even in those areas in which we have grown, there is always need for further growth. Paul wrote in his first letter to the Thessalonian Christians that they had been taught by God to love one another and, in fact, they did love all the brothers throughout Macedonia. That is quite a commendation! But Paul was not satisfied. He went on to say, "Yet we urge you, brothers, to do so more and more" (4:9-10). Growth in Christian character is never finished until we go to be with Christ and are transformed completely into His likeness.

Growth in godly character not only is progressive and always unfinished, it is absolutely necessary for spiritual survival. If we are not growing in godly character, we are regressing; in the spiritual life we never stand still. The word *train* in Paul's admonition to Timothy, "Train yourself to be godly," occurs only four times in the New Testament: 1 Timothy 4:7, Hebrews 5:14 and 12:11, and 2 Peter 2:14. In three of those instances, the result of such training is positive and God-honoring.

But consider the fourth passage, 2 Peter 2:14. The context is Peter's sharp denunciation of and warning against false teachers. He refers to them as "experts in greed." The word *expert* is the same word translated in the other three passages as "train." In fact, the English Standard Version renders it, "They have hearts trained in greed."

The implication of Peter's use of the word *train* is very sober-ing. It is possible to train ourselves in the wrong direction! That is what these false teachers had done. They had *practiced* greed so well that they had become experts in it — they had trained their hearts in greed!

So there is a sense in which we are growing in our character every day. The question is, in which direction are we growing? Are we growing toward godly character or ungodly character? Are we growing in love or selfishness, in harshness or patience, in greed or generosity, in honesty or dishonesty, in purity or impurity? Every day we are training ourselves in one direction or the other by the thoughts we think, the words we say, the actions we take, and the deeds we do.

This sense of progression in character, in either one direc-tion or the other, is also taught in Romans 6:19. Paul refers to the Roman Christians' former bondage to *ever-increasing wickedness*. They were well on their way to becoming experts in wickedness. But now, says Paul, having been freed from the slavery of sin, they are to offer their bodies in slavery to righteousness *leading to holiness*. Righteousness refers here to obedience to God, specific "right actions." Holiness refers to the state or character resulting from those actions; right actions, or obedience, leads to holiness. Of course, both the actions and the character are the result of the working of the Holy Spirit, but He works as we work, and we are able to work because He is at work in us.

The relationship between conduct and character is an inti-mate one. In the form of repeated actions over time, conduct produces character. That is the teaching of 2 Peter 2:14 and Romans 6:19. But it is also true that character determines actions. What we do, we become. What we are, we do. This truth can be illustrated by a circle formed by two curved arrows feeding into each other.

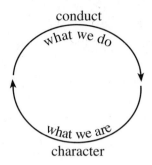

conduct
what we do
what we are
character

Conduct is always feeding character, but character is also always feeding conduct. Paul's experience while shipwrecked on the island of Malta furnishes a good example of this relationship. The islanders built the refugees a fire because of the rain and cold. Luke relates in Acts 28 that Paul gathered a pile of brushwood, and, as he put it on the fire, a snake came out of the brushwood and fastened itself on Paul's hand. Under the adverse circumstances of shipwreck, why would Paul have gone about gathering fuel for a fire built and tended by someone else? Why didn't he just stand by the fire and warm himself? He didn't because it was his character to serve (see Acts 20:33-35 and 1 Thessalonians 2:7-9). He had learned well the lesson Jesus taught us when He washed His disciples' feet. Because it was Paul's character to serve, he gathered the brushwood instinctively. He probably did not even think about it. He just did what his servant character dictated at the moment.

Because conduct determines character, and character determines conduct, it is vitally important — extremely necessary — that we practice godliness every day. That is why Peter says, "Make every effort to add to your faith . . . godliness" (2 Peter 1:5-6). There can be no letup in our pursuit of godly character. Every day that we are not practicing godliness we are being conformed to the world of ungodliness around us.

Granted, our practice of godliness is imperfect and falls far short of the biblical standard. Nevertheless, let us press on to know Christ and to be like Him.

EXERCISES FOR PRACTICE AND DISCUSSION

1. Why is devotion to God the only acceptable motive for actions that please Him?

2. Over the past day, how strong a motivation for your actions has each of the following been?

    > Devotion to God
    > Concern for your reputation
    > The desire to feel good about yourself
    > The habit of living by the ethics you grew up with
    > The desire for security or comfort
    > The desire for status
    > The desire to feel in control or powerful
    > The desire for pleasure

3. Given your personality, which godly character traits are most challenging for you? Which ones are easier?

4. Consider 1 Timothy 4:7-8. What do you think are the essential elements in training oneself to be godly?

5. Pray Psalm 119:33-37. Spend time over it, and ask God to show you areas of your life in which you need to set aside dependence upon your own wisdom and strength of character and draw all that you need from Christ through faith in Him.

6. How can you take responsibility for developing godly character this week? What do you need to do?

CHAPTER TWO

Devotion to God

Who will not fear you, O Lord,
and bring glory to your name?
For you alone are holy.
All nations will come and worship before you,
for your righteous acts have been revealed.

REVELATION 15:4

Through the prophet Ezekiel, the Lord told Israel that one day the people would gain a new attitude: "I will give you a new heart and put a new spirit in you" (Ezekiel 36:26). John Owen calls this new attitude "the habitual inclination of [the] heart unto the life of God."[1] The New Testament word for godliness, in its original meaning, conveys the idea of a personal attitude toward God that results in actions that are pleasing to God.[2]

This personal attitude is what we call devotion to God. But it is always *devotion in action*. It is not just a warm, emotional feeling about God — the kind of feeling we may get while singing some grand old hymn of praise or a modern-day chorus of worship. Nor is devotion to God merely a time of private Bible reading and prayer, a practice we sometimes call "devotions." Although this practice is vitally important to a godly person, we must not think of it as defining devotion for us.

The attitude of devotion to God is composed of three essential elements:

- The fear of God
- The love of God
- The desire for God

From this godward attitude arises the character and conduct that we usually think of as godliness. So often we try to develop Christian character and conduct without taking the time to develop God-centered devotion. We try to please God without taking the time to walk with Him and develop a relationship with Him. This is impossible to do.

Consider the exacting requirements of a godly lifestyle as expounded by the saintly William Law. Law uses the word *devotion* in a broader sense to mean all that is involved in godliness — actions as well as attitude:

> Devotion signifies a life given, or devoted to God. He therefore is the devout [godly] man, who lives no longer to his own will, or the way and spirit of the world, but to the sole will of God, who considers God in everything, who serves God in everything, who makes all the parts of his common life, parts of piety [godliness], by doing everything in the name of God, and under such rules as are conformable to his Glory.[3]

Note the totality of godliness over one's entire life in Law's description of the godly person. Nothing is excluded. God is at the center of his thoughts. His most ordinary duties are done with an eye to God's glory. In Paul's words to the Corinthians, whether the godly person eats or drinks or whatever he does, he does it all for the glory of God.

Now it is obvious that such a God-centered lifestyle cannot be developed and maintained apart from a solid foundation of devotion to God. Only a strong personal relationship with the living God can keep such a commitment from becoming oppressive and legalistic. John writes that God's commands are not burdensome (see 1 John 5:3); a godly life is not wearisome, but this is true only because a godly person is first of all devoted to God. This devotion is the only motivation for Christian behavior that is pleasing to God.

This motivation is what separates the godly person from the moral person, or the benevolent person, or the zealous person. The godly person is moral, benevolent, and zealous because of such a devotion to God. And his life takes on a dimension that reflects the very stamp of God.

Let's consider the three essential elements of devotion: the fear of God, the love of God, and the desire for God. Think of a triangle representing devotion to God, with these three elements as each of its three points.

The fear of God and the love of God form the base of the triangle, while the desire for God is at the apex. As we study these elements individually, we will see that the fear of God and the love of God form the foundation of true devotion to God, while the desire for God is the highest expression of that devotion.

THE GOD-FEARING CHRISTIAN

Professor John Murray says, "The fear of God is the soul of godliness."[4] Yet the fear of God is a concept that seems old-fashioned and antiquated to many modern-day Christians. There was a time when an earnest believer might have been known as a "God-fearing man." Today we would probably be embarrassed by such language. Some seem to think the fear of God is strictly an Old Testament concept that passed away with the revelation of God's love in Christ. After all, doesn't perfect love drive out fear, as John declares in 1 John 4:18?

Although it is true that the concept of the fear of God is treated more extensively in the Old Testament, it would be a mistake to assume that it is not important in the New Testament. One of the blessings of the new covenant is the implanting in believers' hearts of the fear of the Lord. In Jeremiah 32:40, God said, "I will make an everlasting covenant with them: I will never stop doing good to them, and I will inspire them to *fear me*, so that they will never turn away from me" (emphasis added).

"Nothing could be more significant," observes John Murray, "than that the fear of the Lord should be coupled with the comfort of the Holy Spirit as the characteristics of the New Testament church: 'So the church . . . walking in the fear of the Lord and in the comfort of the Holy Spirit [was] multiplied' (Acts 9:31, ESV)."[5] Paul and Peter both use the fear of the Lord as a motive to holy and righteous living.[6] The example of the Lord Jesus Himself, of whom Isaiah said, "He will delight in the fear of the LORD" (11:3), should put the question beyond all doubt. If Jesus in His humanity delighted in the fear of God, surely we need to give serious thought to cultivating this attitude in our lives.

Some of the aversion to the phrase "fear of God" may be due to a misunderstanding of its meaning. The Bible uses the term "fear of God" in two distinct ways: that of anxious dread, and that of veneration, reverence, and awe. Fear as anxious dread is produced by the realization of God's impending judgment upon sin. When Adam sinned, he hid from God because he was afraid. Although this aspect of the fear of God should characterize every unsaved person who lives each day as an object of God's wrath, it seldom does. Paul's concluding indictment of ungodly mankind was, "There is no fear of God before their eyes" (Romans 3:18).

The Christian has been delivered from fear of the wrath of God (see 1 John 4:18). But the Christian has not been delivered from the *discipline* of God against his sinful conduct, and in this sense he still fears God. He works out his salvation with fear and trembling (see Philippians 2:12); he lives his life as a stranger here in reverent fear (see 1 Peter 1:17).

For the child of God, however, the primary meaning of the fear of God is veneration and honor, reverence and awe. Murray says this fear is the soul of godliness.[7] It is the attitude that elicits from our hearts adoration and love, reverence and honor. It focuses not upon the wrath of God but upon the majesty, holiness, and transcendent glory of God. It may be likened to the awe an ordinary but loyal citizen would feel in the close presence of his earthly king, though such awe for an earthly potentate can only distantly approximate the awe we should feel toward God, the blessed and only Ruler, the King of kings and Lord of lords.

The angelic beings of Isaiah's vision in chapter 6 demonstrated this awe when, with two of their wings, they covered their faces in the presence of the exalted Lord. We see this same awe in Isaiah himself and in Peter when they each realized they were in the presence of a holy God. We see it most vividly in the reaction of the beloved disciple John in Revelation 1:17 when he saw his Master in all of His heavenly glory and majesty and fell at His feet as though dead.

It is impossible to be devoted to God if one's heart is not filled with the fear of God. It is this profound sense of veneration and honor, reverence and awe, that draws forth from our hearts the worship and adoration that characterizes true devotion to God. The reverent, godly Christian sees God first in His transcendent glory, majesty, and holiness before seeing Him in His love, mercy, and grace.

There is a healthy tension that exists in the godly person's heart between the reverential awe of God in His glory and the childlike confidence in God as heavenly Father. Without this tension, a Christian's filial confidence can easily degenerate into presumption.

One of the more serious sins of Christians today may well be the almost flippant familiarity with which we often address God in prayer. None of the godly men of the Bible ever adopted the casual manner we often do. They always addressed God with reverence. The same writer who tells us that "we have confidence to enter the Most Holy Place," the throne room of God, also tells us that we should "worship God acceptably with reverence and awe, for our God is a consuming fire" (Hebrews 10:19; 12:28-29). The same Paul who tells us that the Holy Spirit dwelling within us causes us to cry, "*Abba*, Father," also tells us that this same God lives in "unapproachable light" (Romans 8:15 and 1 Timothy 6:16).

In our day, we must begin to recover a sense of awe and profound reverence for God. We must begin to view Him once again in the infinite majesty that alone belongs to Him who is the Creator and Supreme Ruler of the entire universe. There is an infinite gap in worth and dignity between God the Creator and man the creature, even though man has been created in the image of God. The fear of God is a heartfelt recognition of this gap — not a put-down of man but an exaltation of God.

Even the redeemed in heaven fear the Lord. In Revelation 15:3-4, they sing triumphantly the song of Moses the servant of God and the song of the Lamb:

> Great and marvelous are your deeds,
> Lord God Almighty.
>> Just and true are your ways,
> King of the ages.
>> Who will not fear you, O Lord,
>> and bring glory to your name?
> For you alone are holy.
>> All nations will come
>> and worship before you,
>> for your righteous acts have been revealed.

Note the focus of their veneration upon God's attributes of power, justice, and holiness. It is these attributes, which particularly set forth the majesty of God, that should elicit from our hearts a reverence for Him. This same reverence was drawn forth from the children of Israel when they saw the great power the Lord displayed against the Egyptians. Exodus 14:31 says, "The people feared the LORD and put their trust in him and in Moses his servant." Along with Moses, they sang a song of worship and gratitude. The heart of that song is found in 15:11: "Who among the gods is like you, O LORD? Who is like you — majestic in holiness, awesome in glory, working wonders?" To fear God is to confess His absolute uniqueness — to acknowledge His majesty, holiness, awesomeness, glory, and power.

Words fail us to describe the infinite glory of God portrayed in the Bible. And even that portrayal is dim and vague, for now we see but a poor reflection of Him. But one day we will see Him face-to-face, and then we will fear Him in the fullest sense of that word. No wonder, then, that with that day in view, Peter tells us to live holy and godly lives now. God is in the process of preparing us for heaven, to dwell with Him for eternity. So He desires that we grow in both holiness and godliness. He wants us to be like Him and to reverence and adore Him for all eternity. We must be learning to do this now.

In our day, we seem to have magnified the love of God almost to the exclusion of the fear of God. Because of this preoccupation, we are not honoring God and reverencing Him as we should. We should magnify the love of God, but although we revel in His love and mercy, we must never lose sight of His majesty and His holiness.

Not only will a right concept of the fear of God cause us to worship God aright, it will also regulate our conduct. As John Murray says, "What or whom we worship determines our behavior."[8] The Reverend Albert N. Martin has said that the essential ingredients of the fear of God are (1) correct concepts of the character of God, (2) a pervasive sense of the presence of God, and (3) a constant awareness of our obligation to God.[9] If we have some comprehension of God's infinite holiness and His hatred of sin, coupled with this pervasive sense of God's presence in all of our actions, yes, even our thoughts, then such a fear of God must influence and regulate our conduct. Just as obedience to the Lord is an indication of our love for Him, so is it also a proof of our fear of God. "[You shall] fear the LORD your God as long as you live by keeping all his decrees and commands" (Deuteronomy 6:2).

Leviticus 19 contains a series of laws and regulations for the nation of Israel to observe in the Promised Land. It is the chapter from which Jesus quoted the well-known second commandment of love, "Love your neighbor as yourself" (verse 18; see also Matthew 22:39). The expression "I am the LORD" or "I am the LORD your God" appears sixteen times in Leviticus 19. Through this frequent repetition of His sacred name, God reminds the people of Israel that their obedience to His laws and regulations is to flow out of a reverence and fear of Him.

The fear of God should provide a primary motivation for, as well as result in, obedience to Him. If we truly reverence God, we will obey Him, because every act of disobedience is an affront to His dignity and majesty.

GRIPPED BY GOD'S LOVE

Only the God-fearing Christian can truly appreciate the love of God. He or she sees the infinite gulf between a holy God and a sinful creature, and the love that bridged that gulf through the death of the Lord Jesus Christ. God's love for us is many-faceted, but He supremely demonstrated it by sending His Son to die for our sins. All other aspects of His love are secondary and in fact are made possible for us through the death of Christ.

The apostle John says, "God is love" (1 John 4:8). He explains this statement by saying,

> This is how God showed his love among us: He sent his one and only Son into the world that we might live through him. This is love: not that we loved God, but that he loved us and sent his Son as an atoning sacrifice for our sins. (1 John 4:9-10)

The New International Version of the Bible gives as a marginal rendering for "atoning sacrifice" the phrase, "as the one who would turn aside his wrath, taking away" our sins.

The truly godly person never forgets that he was at one time an object of God's holy and just wrath. He never forgets that Christ Jesus came into the world to save sinners, and he feels along with Paul that he is himself the worst of sinners. But then as he looks to the cross, he sees that Jesus was his atoning sacrifice. He sees that Jesus bore his sins in His own body and that the wrath of God — the wrath that he, a sinner, should have borne — was expended completely and totally upon the Holy Son of God. And in this view of Calvary, he sees the love of God.

The love of God has no meaning apart from Calvary, and Calvary has no meaning apart from the holy and just wrath of God. Jesus did not die just to give us peace and a purpose in life; He died to save us from the wrath of God. He died to reconcile us to a holy God who was alienated from us because of our sin. He died to ransom us from the penalty of sin — the punishment of everlasting destruction, shut out from the presence of the Lord. He died that we, the just objects of God's wrath, should become, by His grace, heirs of God and co-heirs with Him.

How much we appreciate God's love is conditioned by how deeply we fear Him. The more we see God in His infinite majesty, holiness, and transcendent glory, the more we will gaze with wonder and amazement upon His love poured out at Calvary. But it is also true that the deeper our perception of God's love to us in Christ, the more profound our reverence and awe of Him. We must see God in the glory of all His attributes — His goodness as well as His holiness — if we are to ascribe to Him the glory and honor and reverence that is due Him. The psalmist caught this truth when he said to God, "If you, O LORD, kept a record of sins, O Lord, who could stand? But with you there is forgiveness; therefore you are feared" (Psalm 130:3-4). He worshiped God with reverence and awe because of His forgiveness. In our practice of godliness, then, we must seek to grow both in the fear of God and in an ever-increasing comprehension of the love of God. These two elements together form the foundation of our devotion to God.

This awareness of God's love for us in Christ must be *personalized* in order for it to become one of the solid foundational corners of our "triangle of devotion" to God. It is not enough for me to believe that God loved the world. I must be gripped by the realization that God loves *me*, a specific person. It is this awareness of His individual love that draws out our hearts in devotion to Him.

There was a period in my early Christian life when my concept of God's love was little more than a logical deduction: God loves the world; I am a part of the world; therefore, God loves me. It was as if God's love were a big umbrella to protect us all from His judgment against sin, and I was under the umbrella along with thousands of other people. There was nothing particularly personal about it. Then one day I realized, "God loves *me*! Christ died for *me*."

Our awareness of God's love for us must also be constantly growing. As we mature in our Christian lives, we are increasingly aware of God's holiness and our own sinfulness. In Paul's first letter to Timothy, he reflects upon God's mercy in appointing him to the gospel ministry. He recalls that he once was a blasphemer and a persecutor and a violent man. This description no longer applies to Paul; it is all past tense. But as he continues to reflect upon the grace of God, he slips, almost unconsciously it seems, into the present tense of his experience. "Christ Jesus came into the world to save sinners — of whom I am the worst" (1:15). He is no longer thinking about his past as a persecutor of Christ; now he is thinking about his present daily experience as a believer who falls short of the will of God for him. He doesn't think about other Christians, whom we know were way behind Paul in their devotion to God and their attainment of godly character. Paul never wastes time trying to feel good about himself by comparing himself favorably with less mature Christians. He compares himself with God's standard, and he consequently sees himself as the worst of sinners.

Through this present sense of his sinfulness, Paul sees God's love for him. The more he grows in his knowledge of God's perfect will, the more he sees his own sinfulness and the more he comprehends God's love in sending Christ to die for him. And the more he sees God's love, the more his heart reaches out in adoring devotion to the One who loves him so.

If God's love for us is to be a solid foundation stone of devotion, we must realize that His love is *entirely of grace*, that it rests completely upon the work of Jesus Christ and flows to us through our union with Him. Because of this basis, His love can never change, regardless of what we do. In our daily experience, we have all sorts of spiritual ups and downs — sin, failure, discouragement — all of which tend to make us question God's love. That is because we keep thinking that God's love is somehow conditional. We are afraid to believe His love is based entirely upon the finished work of Christ for us.

Deep down in our souls, we must get hold of the wonderful truth that our spiritual failures do not affect God's love for us one iota — that His love for us does not fluctuate according to our experience. We must be gripped by the truth that we are accepted by God and loved by God for the sole reason that we are united to His beloved Son. As the King James Version translates Ephesians 1:6, "He hath made us accepted in the beloved."

That is why Paul could rejoice so greatly in the love of God. Listen to the triumphant ring of his voice in Romans 8 as he asks these questions:

- "If God is for us, who can be against us?" (verse 31)
- "Who will bring any charge against those whom God has chosen?" (verse 33)
- "Who is he that condemns?" (verse 34)
- "Who shall separate us from the love of Christ?" (verse 35)

Then hear his exultant conclusion as he says, "For I am convinced that . . . [nothing] . . . will be able to separate us from the love of God that is in Christ Jesus our Lord" (verses 38-39).

Does this apprehension of God's personal, unconditional love for us in Christ lead to careless living? Not at all. Rather, such an awareness of His love stimulates in us an increased devotion to Him. And this devotion is active; it is not just a warm, affectionate feeling toward God.

Paul testified that Christ's love for us compelled him to live not for himself but for Him who died for us and rose again (see 2 Corinthians 5:14-15). The word for "compel" that Paul used is a very strong verb. It means to press in on all sides and to impel or force one to a certain course of action. Probably not many Christians can identify with Paul in this depth of his motivation, but this surely should be our goal. This is the constraining force that God's love is intended to have upon us.

John speaks similarly of the constraining force of God's love when he says, "We love because he first loved us" (1 John 4:19). Whether it is love for God or love for other people that John had in mind, both are prompted by the realization of God's love for us.

So we see that devotion to God begins with the fear of God — with a biblical view of His majesty and holiness that elicits a reverence and awe of Him. And then the fear of God leads naturally to an apprehension of the love of God shown us in the atoning death of Jesus Christ. As we contemplate God more and more in His majesty, holiness, and love, we will be progressively led to the apex of the triangle of devotion: the desire for God Himself.

A THIRST FOR GOD

True godliness engages our affections and awakens within us a desire to enjoy God's presence and fellowship. It produces a longing for God Himself. The writer of Psalm 42 vividly expressed this longing when he exclaimed, "As the deer pants for streams of water, so my soul pants for you, O God. My soul thirsts for God, for the living God. When can I go and meet with God?" (verses 1-2). What could be more intense than a hunted deer's thirst for water? The psalmist does not hesitate to use this picture to illustrate the intensity of his own desire for God's presence and fellowship.

David also expresses this intense desire for God: "One thing I ask of the LORD, this is what I seek: that I may dwell in the house of the LORD all the days of my life, to gaze upon the beauty of the LORD and to seek him in his temple" (Psalm 27:4). David yearned intensely for God Himself that he might enjoy His presence and His beauty. Because God is a spirit, His beauty obviously refers not to a physical appearance but to His attributes. David enjoyed dwelling upon the majesty and greatness, the holiness and goodness of God. But David did more than contemplate the beauty of God's attributes; he sought God Himself, for elsewhere he says, "Earnestly I seek you; my soul thirsts for you, my body longs for you" (Psalm 63:1).

The apostle Paul also experienced this longing for God: "I want to know Christ" (Philippians 3:10). The Amplified Bible forcefully catches the intensity of Paul's desire in this passage:

[For my determined purpose is] that I may know Him — that I may progressively become more deeply and intimately acquainted with Him, perceiving and recognizing and understanding [the wonders of His person] more strongly and more clearly.

This is the heartbeat of the godly person. As he contemplates God in the awesomeness of His infinite majesty, power, and holiness, and then as he dwells upon the riches of His mercy and grace poured out at Calvary, his heart is captivated by this One who could love him so. He is satisfied with God alone, but he is never satisfied with his present experience of God. He always yearns for more.

Perhaps this idea of a desire for God sounds strange to many Christians today. We understand the thought of serving God, of being busy in His work. We may even have a "quiet time," when we read the Bible and pray. But the idea of longing for God Himself, of wanting to deeply enjoy His fellowship and His presence, may seem a bit too mystical, almost bordering on fanaticism. We prefer our Christianity to be more practical.

Yet who could be more practical than Paul? Who was more involved in the struggles of daily living than David? Still, with all their responsibilities, both Paul and David yearned to experience more fellowship with the living God. The Bible, from its earliest pages right through to the end, indicates that this is God's plan for us. In the third chapter of Genesis, God walks in the garden, calling out for Adam that He might have fellowship with him. In Revelation 21, when John sees the vision of the new Jerusalem coming down from heaven, he hears the voice of God say, "Now the dwelling of God is with men, and he will live with them" (verse 3). For all of eternity, God plans to have fellowship with His people.

And during our present day, Jesus still says to us, as He did to the church at Laodicea, "Here I am! I stand at the door and knock. If anyone hears my voice and opens the door, I will come in and eat with him, and he with me" (Revelation 3:20). In the culture of John's day, to share a meal meant to have fellowship, so Jesus is inviting us to open our hearts to Him that we may fellowship with Him. He desires that we come to know Him better; therefore, the desire and yearning for God is something that He plants within our hearts.

In the life of the godly person, this desire for God produces an aura of warmth. Godliness is never austere and cold. Such an idea comes from a false sense of legalistic morality that is erroneously called godliness. The person who spends time with God radiates His glory in a manner that is always warm and inviting, never cold and forbidding.

This longing for God also produces a desire to glorify God and to please Him. In the same breath, Paul expresses the desire to know Christ as well as to be like Him. This is God's ultimate objective for us and is the object of the Spirit's work in us. In Isaiah 26:9, the prophet proclaims his desire for the Lord in words very similar to the psalmist's: "My soul yearns for you in the night; in the morning my spirit longs for you." Note that immediately before this expression of desire for the Lord, Isaiah expresses a desire for His glory: "Your name and renown are the desire of our hearts" (verse 8). Renown has to do with one's reputation, fame, and eminence — or in God's case, His glory. The prophet could not separate in his heart his desire for God's glory and his desire for God Himself. These two yearnings go hand in hand.

This is devotion to God — the fear of God, which is an attitude of reverence and awe, veneration and honor toward Him, coupled with an apprehension deep within our souls of the love of God for us, demonstrated preeminently in the atoning death of Christ. These two attitudes complement and rein-force each other, producing within our souls an intense desire for this One who is so awesome in His glory and majesty and yet so condescending in His love and mercy.

EXERCISES FOR PRACTICE AND DISCUSSION

1. To what extent would you say God is at the center of your thoughts? In a typical day, do you think of Him occasionally? Frequently? Constantly?

2. Who or what has dominated your thoughts over the past day? Why is that?

3. What role does each of the following play in your life? What, if anything, have you done recently that was motivated by one or more of these?

> The fear of God
> The love of God
> The desire for God

4. How can you cultivate a healthy fear of God?

5. How can you deepen your awareness of God's love for you?

6. Why should desire for God naturally well up in you?

7. Choose one of these passages for meditation:

> Isaiah 6:1-7 (the fear of God)
> Romans 8:31-39 (the love of God)
> Psalm 63:1-3 (the desire for God)

By meditation I mean the practice of reflecting slowly on a passage, phrase by phrase. Let the passage ask you questions, and ask God questions about the passage. Stop at things that strike you as significant. What is God saying to your mind, emotions, and will? What is He inviting you to do?

CHAPTER THREE

Humility

For everyone who exalts himself will be humbled,
and he who humbles himself will be exalted.

LUKE 18:14

The fruit of the Spirit is fundamentally relational. Rather than originating with us, it flows to us from our union with Christ, and it flows beyond us to bring us into fellowship with others. The secret of this flow — and of our unity with God and others — is *humility*. Sinclair B. Ferguson writes:

> [The] mind that we have in union with Christ and in the fellowship of the Spirit is to be the mindset we exercise with respect to one another, counting each other of greater importance than we count ourselves.[1]

Before we move on to the nine traits the apostle Paul calls the fruit of the Spirit, we must look at humility, for without humility we cannot hope to cultivate the rest of the fruit. Two passages from the book of Isaiah show us clearly the esteem with which God views the humble person. We read in Isaiah 57:15,

> For this is what the high and lofty One says —
>> he who lives forever, whose name is holy:
> "I live in a high and holy place,
>> but also with him who is contrite and lowly in
>>> spirit,
> to revive the spirit of the lowly
>> and to revive the heart of the contrite."

And then we read in Isaiah 66:1-2,

> This is what the LORD says:

> "Heaven is my throne
>> and the earth is my footstool.
> Where is the house you will build for me?
>> Where will my resting place be?
> Has not my hand made all these things,
>> and so they came into being?"
>> declares the LORD.
> "This is the one I esteem:
>> he who is humble and contrite in spirit,
>> and trembles at my word."

Not only does God commend humility in His people, our Lord displayed it in His humanity. "And being found in appearance as a man, he humbled himself and became obedient to death — even death on a cross!" (Philippians 2:8). Jesus Christ exemplified humility in its utmost through His death for us. But He also exemplified humility throughout His life. He was born in the very humblest of circumstances; He was obedient to His earthly parents; He called people to Himself as one who was "gentle and humble in heart"; He said, "I am among you as one who serves"; He washed the disciples' feet on the very night of His betrayal; and He taught, "He who humbles himself will be exalted" (see Luke 2:7,51; Matthew 11:29; Luke 22:27; see John 13:5; Luke 14:11). If we ever wonder whether humility is technically a *godlike* trait (as we view God in His majesty), we certainly cannot question that it is a *Christlike* trait. And we are to be imitators of how He lived out His human life on earth.

The promises of God toward the truly humble are almost breathtaking. The infinitely high and lofty One who lives forever promises to dwell with them, to esteem them, to give them grace, to lift them up, and to exalt them (see Isaiah 57:15; 66:2; James 4:6; 1 Peter 5:6; Luke 18:14). Humility opens the way to all other godly character traits. It is the soil in which the other traits of the fruit of the Spirit grow.

Humility manifests itself in our relationships — to God, to ourselves, to others. We are to be humble toward God and His Word, humble in regard to trials and blessings that come our way or abilities and achievements with which we are blessed, and humble toward other people. Humility is the proper attitude with which to approach all these relationships and circumstances. Like love, it defies adequate definition; it can only be described and understood as it is applied to everyday living.

HUMILITY BEFORE GOD

Humility toward God is akin to the fear of God: It begins with a high view of God's person. As we see God in His majesty, awesomeness, and holiness, we are humbled before Him. In every occasion in the Scriptures in which man was privileged to view God in His glory, he was brought low or humbled in the presence of Him. Moses bowed to the ground and worshiped; Isaiah cried, "Woe is me!"; Ezekiel fell face down; John fell at His feet as though dead. Even the four living creatures and the twenty-four elders in heaven of Revelation fell down before the throne of the glorified Lamb.

Humility in every area of life, in every relationship with other people, begins with a right concept of God as the One who is infinite and eternal in His majesty and holiness. We are to humble ourselves under God's mighty hand, approaching every relationship and every circumstance in reference to Him. When relationships with people are good and circumstances are favorable, we are to humbly receive these blessings from His gracious hand. When people are mistreating us and circumstances are difficult, we are to humbly accept them as from an infinitely wise and loving heavenly Father.

This humility before God is basic to all our relationships in life. We cannot begin to experience humility in any other relationship until we experience a deep and profound humility in our attitude toward God. When we are conscious of our (sinful) creature relationship to an infinitely majestic and holy God, we will not wish to selfishly compare ourselves with others. And to the extent that our awareness of our lowly place before God is an abiding one, we will avoid the temptations of pride and competition.

TREMBLING AT HIS WORD

The person who is truly humble before God is also humble before God's Word. God says He esteems the person who is humble and contrite in spirit and who trembles at His Word. When King Josiah heard the words of the Book of the Law, he tore his robes, saying, "Great is the LORD's anger that burns against us because our fathers have not obeyed the words of this book" (2 Kings 22:13). Josiah realized that the Word of God was the expression of the will of God, that it was to be obeyed, and that failure to obey would incur the judgment of God. Because Josiah trembled at the Word of God, his heart was responsive, he humbled himself, he acknowledged the sin of his people, and God heard him. He did not dispute the Word of God; he simply obeyed it.

We also must develop this kind of humility toward the Bible. As we search the Scriptures, we must allow them to search us, to sit in judgment upon our character and conduct. We must treat the Scriptures not only as a source of knowledge about God but also as the expression of His will for our daily lives. As the familiar statement goes, "The Bible was given not just to increase our knowledge, but to guide our conduct." Far too often it seems we approach the Bible just to increase our knowledge of the facts of the Bible. We do need to increase our spiritual knowledge, but it should be for the purpose of obeying God's will. Paul prayed that God would fill the Colossian Christians with the knowledge of His will so that they might live a life worthy of the Lord and please Him in every way.

Not only must we develop a spirit of humility toward the Bible in regard to our *conduct*, we must also develop such a spirit in regard to our *doctrines*. We evangelicals are not noted for our humility about our doctrines — our beliefs about what the Bible teaches in various areas of theology. Whatever position we take in a specific area of theology, we tend to feel that our position is airtight and that anyone holding a different view is altogether wrong. We tend to be quite impatient with anyone who differs from us. Ironically, the more our views come from the teachings of someone else instead of from the Bible itself, the more rigidly we tend to hold those views.

It is one thing to be persuaded that what we believe is correct as we understand the Scriptures; it is quite another to believe that our views are *always* correct. Twice in my life I have had to make significant changes in my doctrines as a result of additional understanding of the Scriptures. This is not to suggest that we are to be wishy-washy in our beliefs so that we are "blown here and there by every wind of teaching" (Ephesians 4:14) but that we are to hold our beliefs in a spirit of true humility. We must remind ourselves that God has not seen fit to make our minds, or even a particular church, the depository of the sum total of His teaching.

At one time in His ministry, Jesus prayed, "I praise you, Father, Lord of heaven and earth, because you have hidden these things from the wise and learned, and revealed them to little children. Yes, Father, for this was your good pleasure" (Luke 10:21). Commenting on this passage, Norvel Geldenhuys aptly remarks,

> The contrast pointed by the Savior is not that between "educated" and "non-educated" but between those who imagine themselves to be wise and sensible — and those who live under the profound impression that by their own insight and their own reasonings they are utterly powerless to understand the truths of God and to accept them.[2]

May God help us to be humble enough toward the Scriptures to be found in that group that Jesus called "little children."

HERE BY THE GRACE OF GOD

When a believer is truly humble before God and His Word, he will also be humble about his own gifts, abilities, and attainments. He will realize and gratefully acknowledge that all that he is and all that he has comes from the hand of God.

This aspect of humility actually begins with our understanding of personal salvation. All evangelicals agree we are saved solely by the grace of God, apart from any works of our own. But do we believe, even in some undefined way, that we did contribute something to our salvation — something that implies that we were a little bit wiser, or a little smarter, or a little more responsive to God than others?

Some time ago, I read a statement in which the writer said he realized that the only difference between himself and another group of people was that perhaps he had a little more reliance upon the grace of God. I am sure the writer meant this as an expression of humility, but it left me uncomfortable. Somehow I cannot imagine the apostle Paul finding any distinguishing difference in himself, even a little more reliance upon the grace of God. Instead, I find him saying, "Christ Jesus came into the world to save sinners — of whom I am the worst" (1 Timothy 1:15). Paul never compared himself favorably to the unbelievers around him. He was too overwhelmed with the fact that the grace of God was sufficient to reach even him.

Our attitude of humility in regard to our salvation should carry over to a recognition that any of our abilities and achievements are equally a result of God's grace. In his first epistle to the Corinthian Christians, Paul minces no words on this subject: "For who makes you different from anyone else? What do you have that you did not receive? And if you did receive it, why do you boast as though you did not?" (4:7). Every ability and every advantage we have comes from God and has been given to us as a stewardship to be used in serving Him. For some time after I went into full-time Christian work and was living on a mere subsistence income, I often struggled with thoughts of how much money I could have been making if I had followed the profession I was trained for in college. Finally, I began to realize that it was God who had given me the advantage of a good education and that I was not doing Him a favor by being in His service full-time. All that I had came from Him and was to be used for His glory.

Paul refused to take the credit for his abilities or even his diligent labors. Again in his first letter to the Corinthians, he declares, "By the grace of God I am what I am, and his grace to me was not without effect. No, I worked harder than all of them — yet not I, but the grace of God that was with me" (15:10). This passage used to puzzle me. It seemed as if Paul was trying to be both humble and proud. How could anyone dare to state publicly that he had worked harder than all of the other apostles? But then I realized that Paul was ascribing even his hard work to the grace of God. Sometimes we hear some tired Christian describing how hard he or she has worked in the service of God, teaching Sunday school for ten years straight, or sponsoring a difficult junior high youth group, or being one of the faithful few at Wednesday night prayer meeting. Perhaps we ourselves have been one of those tired Christians. If so, let's remember to credit our hard work and faithful labors strictly to the grace of God.

We should ascribe any attainments, whether secular or spiritual, to the grace of God. When Moses was giving final instructions to the children of Israel prior to entering the Promised Land, he specifically warned them against the pride that comes with taking credit for successes:

> You may say to yourself, 'My power and the strength of my hands have produced this wealth for me.' But remember the LORD your God, for it is he who gives you the ability to produce wealth, and so confirms his covenant, which he swore to your forefathers, as it is today. (Deuteronomy 8:17-18)

Paul was just as emphatic about spiritual success when he wrote, "So neither he who plants nor he who waters is anything, but only God, who makes things grow" (1 Corinthians 3:7). The prophet Isaiah succinctly expressed the attitude we are to have toward accomplishments when he said, "LORD . . . all that we have accomplished you have done for us" (26:12).

While writing this chapter, I had occasion to express appreciation to a fellow church member for a job well done. I liked his simple, humble response: "It was the Lord who did it." Humility with regard to ourselves, then, consists in ascribing all that we are, all that we have, and all that we have accomplished to the God who gives us grace.

SUBMISSION, SERVICE, AND HONOR

A believer who is humble before God will also be humble toward other people. One way this humility expresses itself is in mutual submission to one another. Paul instructs us, "Submit to one another out of reverence for Christ" (Ephesians 5:21). Peter likewise says, "Clothe yourselves with humility toward one another" (1 Peter 5:5), and James tells us that submissiveness is characteristic of the wisdom that comes from heaven (see James 3:17). What does it mean to submit to one another? Does it mean always giving in to others' demands or opinions? Not at all. It means to submit to *instruction* as well as *correction* from other believers; to be teachable or to be humble enough to admit we have erred when another believer corrects us.

Apollos and Peter are beautiful examples of men who submitted themselves to other believers. Apollos submitted himself to others' instruction. Luke tells us that Apollos was a learned man, with a thorough knowledge of the Scriptures, who had been instructed in the way of the Lord and who spoke with great fervor and taught about Jesus accurately. Apollos was obviously a gifted and capable man and apparently a "full-time Christian worker," but he had one defect: His knowledge about Christ was accurate but incomplete; he knew only the baptism of John. When Priscilla and Aquila, a godly "lay" couple in the church at Ephesus, heard Apollos, they invited him to their home and explained the way of God more adequately (see Acts 18:24-26). It is evident that Apollos received their instruction because shortly thereafter, when Apollos wanted to go on to minister to the churches in Achaia, the church at Ephesus not only encouraged him but also wrote a letter to the Achaian Christians telling them to welcome him.

What a commentary on the humility of Apollos! What a sermon by example on what it means to submit to one another! Apollos was a capable, gifted minister, yet he was not above receiving instruction from Priscilla and Aquila. (It is not too hard to imagine with what gentleness and consideration Priscilla and Aquila must have instructed Apollos. That is the other side of submission to one another — but more about that when we get to the trait of gentleness in chapter 10.)

Peter provides us with an example of submitting to the correction of another believer. When Peter came to Antioch, Paul found it necessary to rebuke Peter because of his hypocrisy in regard to the Gentile Christians. Not only was Paul's rebuke severe, it was done openly before the other believers. The Scriptures do not tell us what Peter's reaction was, but apparently Peter did not harbor any resentment toward Paul. In one of his own letters, he later refers to Paul as "our dear brother" and speaks of Paul's letters as Scripture — that is, as part of the divinely inspired writings of the Word of God (see 2 Peter 3:15-16). Peter had evidently accepted Paul's rebuke. He had humbly submitted himself to the correction of another believer, even though that believer was "younger in the Lord" than he.

There is no question that submission to the unsolicited teaching or correction of others is difficult for our naturally proud hearts. But the context of Paul's instruction on mutual submission in Ephesians 5 indicates it is one of the evidences of being filled with the Spirit. Though not mentioned explicitly in Galatians 5:22-23, humility is surely a fruit of the Spirit, the result of His ministry in our hearts. But this ministry does not occur without deliberate, conscious effort on our part. The Spirit does not make us humble; He enables us to humble ourselves in these difficult situations.

Although submission is probably the most difficult application of humility toward others, it is by no means the only one. A very common occasion for showing humility is through *serving one another*. In this area, Jesus is our greatest teacher and pacesetter. The foremost example is His washing the disciples' feet on the night of His betrayal, but Jesus' whole life was one of serving others. He said He did not come to be served but to serve; He went around doing good for others. He even seems to indicate that He will still be serving us in eternity (see Luke 12:37), as incredible as that may seem.[3]

In addition to the example He set for us, Jesus also taught us by precept the importance of serving one another. He indicated that true greatness in the kingdom of God does not consist in position but in serving one another, and He promised blessing to those who followed His example in serving others.

This demonstration of humility in serving others also requires the grace of God. Peter tells us that those who serve "should do it with the strength God provides, so that in all things God may be praised through Jesus Christ" (1 Peter 4:11). We all know people, even unbelievers, who seem to be natural servants. They are always serving others one way or another. But God does not get the glory; they do. It is *their* reputation that is enhanced. But when we, natural servants or not, serve in dependence upon the grace of God with the strength He supplies, God is glorified.

Dependence upon the grace of God not only results in God being glorified but it also makes it possible for those of us who are not natural servants to practice this aspect of humility. His grace is sufficient for all of our needs, whatever they may be. We can, by His enablement, *learn* to serve one another.

A third way we demonstrate humility is by *honoring* one another. Paul says in Romans 12:10, "Honor one another above yourselves," and in Philippians 2:3, "Consider others better than yourselves." We are to place the other person above ourselves in matters of position, concerns, or needs.

Jesus rebuked the Pharisees for seeking the places of honor at a feast, telling them to seek out the lowest place instead. We may condemn the childish self-seeking of the Pharisees, but how about our own behavior? Do we maneuver for first place in line or for the best seats at public meetings? Do we frequently assert ourselves at the expense of others, or do we consider their interests as well as our own?

If we are to experience the blessings promised to the humble, we must work out this humility in our daily relationships with others. We must learn to submit to one another, to serve one another, and to honor or prefer one another above ourselves. Remember, the Spirit does not make us humble, but He enables us to humble ourselves. We must *learn* humility, just as Paul learned contentment, but in our efforts we are assured of the same enabling power he experienced (see Philippians 4:11-13).

PRACTICING HUMILITY

Here are some practical suggestions for learning humility. Begin by renewing your mind. The best way to do this is to memorize one or more passages of Scripture, choosing those you believe address most directly your areas of greatest need.

As we memorize and then meditate on Scriptures in this way, the Holy Spirit transforms us inwardly, changing our values; for example, we may begin to place greater importance on putting others ahead of ourselves. The Holy Spirit will also use these

Scriptures we have memorized to convict us in specific situations when we fail to live up to our new values.

Confess any prideful ways as the Holy Spirit convicts you and pray for sensitivity to seeing yourself as God does. Also pray for the Holy Spirit to change you inwardly.

Finally, take whatever specific steps are necessary in order to obey God's direction to humble yourself. We are to humble ourselves before God. The word *humble,* when used in this way, is an action verb. We are to do something. It may be a specific act of putting another first, such as in a supermarket checkout line or in an opportunity for a choice job position. It might even be as drastic as telling our friends we have taken the credit for success that rightfully belongs to God. Whatever the area of humility we need to work on, it is important we do so in dependence upon Him who is at work in us.

EXERCISES FOR PRACTICE AND DISCUSSION

1. Isaiah 57:15 and James 4:6 make strong promises about how God relates to humble versus proud people. Why do you suppose God dwells with and gives grace to humble people?

2. How would you define humility? How is it different from the belief that one is worthless or unlovable?

3. Meditate on Jesus' humility in Philippians 2:3-8. What are some of the things His humility cost Him?

4. How can you cultivate an attitude of humility before God?

5. Read Luke 10:21. What will a humble attitude toward God's Word involve for you?

6. Review the past couple of days, looking for situations in which you were tempted to act in a self-centered way instead of putting others before yourself. What did you do in each case? What do you observe about yourself?

7. Pray for sensitivity to see yourself as God does. Confess any self-centered ways. Pray for the grace to change.

8. Is there a particular biblical passage, perhaps one in this chapter, that would help you develop humility? If so, take some time to meditate on it.

CHAPTER FOUR

Love

And over all these virtues put on love,
which binds them all together in perfect unity.

COLOSSIANS 3:14

When Paul lists those godly traits he calls the fruit of the Spirit, he puts love first — very likely to emphasize its importance. Love is the overall grace from which all the others grow. Indeed, love binds all the other virtues together in perfect unity.

Devotion to God is the only motivation acceptable to God for the development and exercise of Christian character (see chapter 2). But devotion to God finds its outward expression in loving one another. Or to state it another way, our devotion to God is validated by our love for other people. As the apostle John puts it, "For anyone who does not love his brother, whom he has seen, cannot love God, whom he has not seen. And he has given us this command: Whoever loves God must also love his brother" (1 John 4:20-21).

We cannot truly love God without loving one another. To recognize that there is someone I do not love is to say to God, "I do not love you enough to love that person." This is not to deny the reality of spiritual struggle in loving a particular person, because it often exists. I am referring to the attitude of not even wanting to love the person, of being content to allow a lack of love for someone reside in my heart unchecked and unchallenged.

Jesus linked loving God to loving man in Matthew 22:37-40, when He was asked about the greatest commandment in the Law. George Bethune observes of this passage,

> The command to man to "love God with all his heart, and with all his mind, and with all his strength," is followed by a command to "love his neighbor as himself," which could not be, unless love to our neighbor is included in love to God; for how else can we give all our heart to God, and love ourselves and our neighbor too? [1]

Devotion to God is the ultimate motivation for Christian character, but it is also true that love for other believers is the more proximate motivation for the exercise of Christian graces among one another. If we rephrased the virtues of love in 1 Corinthians 13 in terms of motivational statements, they might sound something like this:

- I am patient with you because I love you and want to forgive you.
- I am kind to you because I love you and want to help you.
- I do not envy your possessions or your gifts because I love you and want you to have the best.
- I do not boast about my attainments because I love you and want to hear about yours.
- I am not proud because I love you and want to esteem you before myself.

- I am not rude because I love you and care about your feelings.
- I am not self-seeking because I love you and want to meet your needs.
- I am not easily angered by you because I love you and want to overlook your offenses.
- I do not keep a record of your wrongs because I love you, and "love covers over a multitude of sins" (1 Peter 4:8).

Expressing love in this manner, as a motivational factor, helps us see what Paul had in mind when he said that love binds together all the virtues of Christian character. Love is not so much a character trait as the inner disposition of the soul that produces them all. Bethune says love is "a holy, abiding and vigorous spirit, which rules the whole man, ever directing him to the humble and loving fulfillment of all his duties to God and man."[2] But although love may be more a motivational force than an actual display of Christian virtue, it *always* results in action on our part. Love inclines us and directs us to be kind, to forgive, to give of ourselves to one another. As Peter says to us, "Above all, love each other deeply" (1 Peter 4:8).

GOD IS LOVE

The apostle John makes two statements concerning the essential nature of God: "God is light" (1 John 1:5) and "God is love" (1 John 4:8). Love is defined here not as an action, nor even as a character trait, but as an essential part of God's nature. As Bethune notes, "God was love long before he had made any creatures to be the objects of his love, even from all eternity."[3]

God is infinitely glorious in all His attributes, but the Bible seems to give preeminence to His holiness and to His goodness or love. In Exodus 33, there is an instructive relationship between God's goodness and God's glory. In response to Moses' request, "Now show me your glory," God replies, "I will cause all my goodness to pass in front of you, and I will proclaim my name, the LORD, in your presence" (verses 18-19). Yet in verse 22, God says, "When my glory passes by . . ." It appears from the correlation of verses 18 and 22 that God equates His glory with His goodness. And how does God describe His goodness? Exodus 34:6-7 says, "And he passed in front of Moses, proclaiming, 'The LORD, the LORD, the compassionate and gracious God, slow to anger, abounding in love and faithfulness, maintaining love to thousands, and forgiving wickedness, rebellion and sin.'"

The children of Israel seemed to recognize God's goodness as the expression of His glory. At the dedication of Solomon's temple, according to 2 Chronicles 7:2, the glory of the Lord so filled the temple that the priests could not enter. Then verse 3 tells us,

> When all the Israelites saw the fire coming down and the glory of the LORD above the temple, they knelt on the pavement with their faces to the ground, and they worshiped and gave thanks to the LORD, saying, "He is good; his love endures forever."

Notice the Israelites' response when they saw God's glory: "He is good." God's goodness is the preeminent expression of His glory. If we desire to be godlike and to glorify God in our lives, we must make the cultivation and exercise of love in our hearts an urgent priority. There are three overall prayer requests I make when I pray for myself and others: that I and they would grow in holiness, humility, and love. Of these three, however, love has priority, for if I love God, I will seek to be holy, and if I love other people, I will seek to be humble, putting their interests ahead of mine.

If love to God and to our neighbor should be our highest priority, then it is important for us to know how love expresses itself. First Corinthians 13 is, of course, the most familiar description of love; however, there are two other Scripture passages that seem to sum up the essence of love into two overall traits that will be easily remembered. These passages are 1 John 3:16-18 and 4:7-11.

LOVE GIVES, WHATEVER THE COST

In 1 John 3:16, John says, "This is how we know what love is: Jesus Christ laid down his life for us." The key idea here is that *love gives, even at great cost to itself.* Jesus gave His life for us. John 3:16 tells us that the Father so loved that He gave His only Son to die for us. In Jesus' incarnation and death, both the Father and the Son gave in response to our desperate plight. Nothing but the Savior's incarnation and death would suffice to rescue us. The cost was infinite, but God the Father and God the Son loved us so much they did not hesitate to pay the cost to meet our need.

John says in his epistle that we, too, should give even at great cost to ourselves: We should "lay down our lives for our brothers" (1 John 3:16). In the context of Jesus' sacrifice, John's challenge to us seems overwhelming and impossible — the ultimate act of love. But John's application is very practical and down-to-earth: He asks that we share with our brother in need. However, we are to do this out of pity and compassion, not duty. We are to put our love into practice by meeting our brother's need — even at great cost to ourselves.

There are tremendous needs in the world today, and we Christians ought to be involved in meeting those needs. John is very clear on this point: "If anyone has material possessions and sees his brother in need but has no pity on him, how can the love of God be in him?" (1 John 3:17). Paul tells us that the Macedonian Christians exhibited this kind of love: "Out of the most severe trial, their overflowing joy and their extreme poverty welled up in rich generosity. For I testify that they gave as much as they were able, and even beyond their ability" (2 Corinthians 8:2-3). They gave out of love and at great cost to themselves to meet the material needs of the Christians in Jerusalem, whom they had never even met. We should give to our church and to the work of missions, but we should not overlook the fact that the most well-known passage in the Bible on giving, 2 Corinthians 8–9, has to do with giving to the poor.

And keep in mind that material needs are not the only ones our brother has. Often he needs a listening ear, a word of encouragement, or a helping hand. But to meet those needs requires us to give of ourselves — our time, our attention, and often our heart. This can be more difficult than giving money. Paul says of Timothy, "I have no one else like him, who takes a genuine interest in your welfare" (Philippians 2:20). As he compliments Timothy, Paul adds a striking indictment of others: "For everyone looks out for his own interests, not those of Jesus Christ" (verse 21).

To meet the nonmaterial needs of others costs getting out of ourselves, our concerns, and our interests. We cannot take a genuine interest in the welfare of others, as did Timothy, unless we are willing to become involved in their interests and their concerns. And we cannot do this unless we are willing to forego our own interests. But love willingly pays the price.

LOVE SACRIFICES TO FORGIVE

The second passage in which John instructs us in the meaning of love is 1 John 4:9-11. Immediately following his declaration that "God is love," John says,

> This is how God showed his love among us: He sent his one and only Son into the world that we might live through him. This is love: not that we loved God, but that he loved us and sent his Son as an atoning sacrifice for our sins. Dear friends, since God so loved us, we also ought to love one another.

Once again, John points us to God's sacrifice in sending His Son into the world that we might live through Him. But the central thought is that *God gave in order that He might forgive*. He sent His Son as an atoning sacrifice for our sins. The concept of atonement is best expressed by the marginal reading of the New International Version: "the one who would turn aside his wrath, taking away" our sins. God gave His Son, who took away our sins by bearing in His own body God's wrath, thus turning away that wrath from us. God's justice required that our sin be punished, and forgiveness was impossible as long as justice was unsatisfied. So God gave His Son in order that He might forgive us. He forgave at great cost to Himself.

Now John once again applies God's love to our relationships with one another. He says that because God so loved us, we also ought to love one another. Do we love one another enough to forgive each other, with or without apologies for wrongs done to us? So often we want to exact the last ounce of remorse and repentance from our erring brother before we will even consider forgiving him. But God did not do this. When we were still sinners, still His enemies, He sent His

Son to die for us so that He might forgive us. And John urges us to do likewise.

Forgiveness cost God His Son on the cross, but what does it cost us to forgive one another? Forgiving costs us our sense of justice. We all have this innate sense deep within our souls, but it has been perverted by our selfish, sinful natures. We want to see "justice" done, but the justice we envision satisfies our own interests. We must realize that justice has been done. God is the only rightful administrator of justice in all of creation, and His justice has been satisfied. In order to forgive our brother, we must be satisfied with God's justice and forego the satisfaction of our own.

I recall a personal struggle a number of years ago in loving one of my brothers in Christ. One evening, the Holy Spirit addressed to my mind the rather startling question, "Do you believe I love him just as he is?" I hadn't thought of that before, but I did concede that surely God must love him just as he was, faults and all. And then God pressed this question to my mind, "If I can love him, can you?" God was teaching me to love as He loves, to forgive as He forgives. And love forgives at great cost to itself; it does not demand justice or even changed behavior from its brother.

This forgiving aspect of love enables us to be patient with one another and live at peace with one another. It enables us to deal gently with each other, even when we are sinned against. If we are to grow in the grace of love, we must be ready to forgive, even at great cost to ourselves.

LOVE REACHES OUT

Often in our teaching on love, we stress — and rightly so — that biblical love is not emotions or feelings but rather attitudes and actions that seek the best interests of the other person, regardless of how we feel toward him or her. Vine says, for example, "Christian love . . . is not an impulse from the feelings, it does not always run with the natural inclinations, nor does it spend itself only upon those for whom some affinity is discovered."[4] An illustration from my book *The Pursuit of Holiness* provides an example of this kind of love:

> Suppose you were meditating on 1 Corinthians 13, the great love chapter. As you think about the chapter, you realize the importance of love and you also see the practical outworking of love: Love is patient and kind and does not envy. You ask yourself, "Am I impatient or unkind or envious toward anyone?" As you think about this, you realize you are envious toward Joe at work who seems to be getting all the breaks. You confess this sin to God, being very specific to name Joe and your sinful reaction to his good fortune. You ask God to bless him even more and to give you a spirit of contentment so that you will not continue to envy Joe, but will instead love him. You might memorize 1 Corinthians 13:4 and think about it as you see Joe at work. You even look for ways to help him. Then you do the same thing tomorrow and the next day and the next till finally you see God working a spirit of love in your heart toward Joe.[5]

So love is very much a matter of actions rather than emotions. However, although this emphasis on *acts of love* is certainly necessary, we can sometimes give the impression that love doesn't involve any emotion— that it is entirely an act of the will, of one's duty, regardless of how one feels. We can even promote the "I can love him but I can't like him" type of attitude. The Bible does not support such an unbalanced concept of love.

In describing the Christian's love toward his brother, the Bible uses such expressions as "Love one another deeply, from the heart" (I Peter 1:22) and "Be devoted to one another in brotherly love" (Romans 12:10). Some translations choose such words as *fervently, fondly,* and *affectionately* in the same passages to describe the love Christians ought to have for one another. Three different writers use the expression "brotherly love" or "love as brothers," all indicating that Christian love is to be characterized by an affection that family members have — or ought to have — for one another (see Hebrews 13:1; I Peter 3:8).

All of these passages from the Bible indicate that our emotions are involved. We are to reach out and embrace each other with a deep fervency of spirit, in our hearts if not in actuality. Obviously, such a fervency of spirit cannot substitute for loving actions, but surely it should accompany them. We dare not settle for less.

From the contents of Paul's epistles to the churches, we can safely say that the two churches that caused him the most grief were Corinth and Galatia. Yet sense the emotion in Paul's voice when he writes to the Corinthians, "For I wrote you out of great distress and anguish of heart and with many tears, not to grieve you but to let you know the depth of my love for you" (2 Corinthians 2:4). And to the Galatians he wrote, "My dear children, for whom I am again in the pains of childbirth until Christ is formed in you, how I wish I could be with you now and change my tone, because I am perplexed about you!" (4:19-20). *Distress, anguish, tears,* and *pains of childbirth* are all terms calculated to express the deep emotion of Paul's love toward these people. That their actions made them difficult to love only deepened the intensity of his love for them. And that love was not just an impersonal act of writing them letters of correction in their best interest; he reached out and embraced them even while he rebuked them.

One of the greatest moments of my Christian life occurred one day when I opened my arms and warmly embraced a brother in Christ whom I had somewhat disliked for several years. God had so dealt with me that I finally realized that to think about anyone, *I will love him, but I can't like him* was a great deal less than God's standard of love and was therefore a sinful attitude on my part.

Love is more than a mere act of the will. Going back again to Bethune's definition, love is a *vigorous* spirit that rules the whole man, ever directing him to the humble and loving fulfillment of his duties to God and man. We should do more than just *decide* to do acts of love: we should *desire* to do them. This is not to say we are to do acts of love only when we feel like doing them; it is to say we are not to content ourselves merely with acts of the will, good as those acts may be. We are to lay hold of God in prayer until He gives us that vigorous and loving spirit that delights to reach out and embrace our brother and meet his need or forgive his sin, even if it is at great cost to ourselves.

GROWING IN LOVE

It is obvious that the love we have been considering can be produced in our hearts only by the Spirit of God. Paul wrote to the Thessalonian believers, "You yourselves have been taught by God to love each other" (1 Thessalonians 4:9). Yet just a few words later Paul says, "We urge you, brothers, to [love] more and more" (verse 10). We must review this principle: Godlike character is both the fruit of the Spirit as He works within us and the result of our personal efforts. We are both totally dependent upon His working within us and totally responsible for our own character development. This is an apparent contradiction to our either-or type of thinking, but it is a truth taught over and over in the Scriptures.

How, then, can we fulfill our responsibility to love "more and more"? Recognizing that love is an inner disposition of the soul produced only by the Holy Spirit, what can we do to fulfill our responsibility? First, as we have already seen, the Spirit of God uses His Word to transform us. Therefore, if we want to grow in love, we must saturate our minds with Scriptures that describe love and show its importance to us. First Corinthians 13:1-3, for example, tells us of the emptiness of all knowledge, abilities, and zeal apart from love. First Corinthians 13:4-7 describes love in terms of specific attitudes and actions. Romans 13:8-10 describes love in terms of fulfilling the law of God in our lives. We have already looked at the two passages in 1 John in terms of giving and forgiving. Do you truly want to grow in love? Then you must begin by meditating on some of these love passages.

The second thing we must do is pray for the Holy Spirit to apply His Word to our hearts and to our daily lives. Paul did not just exhort the Thessalonians to grow in love; he looked to the Lord to work in their hearts: "May the Lord make your love increase and overflow for each other and for everyone else, just as ours does for you" (1 Thessalonians 3:12). As we see instances in our lives of failing to love, we should confess them to God, asking Him to help us grow in those specific areas and be more sensitive to such occasions in the future.

Finally, we must obey. We must do those things that love dictates. We must do no harm to our neighbor (see Romans 13:10); we must meet our neighbor's needs and forgive our neighbor's wrongs against us. We must put his interests before our own, and we must reach out and embrace our brother in Christ. But we must do all this in dependence upon the Holy Spirit, who works in us to will and act according to His good purpose.

Does this all sound too methodical? Can we in fact structure love? No; nor can we structure the work of the Holy Spirit in our lives. But we can structure our responsibilities in seeking to grow in love. We can decide to meditate on Scripture — and set aside a time to do it. We can decide to pray over our need to grow in love — and set aside time to do it. We can think of people who need our time, our interest, or our money — and plan to meet those needs. We can admit our failures to love in specific situations and bring those failures to God in confession and dependence upon Him for His help in the future.

All these things we can do, and we *must* do, if we are to grow in the grace of love. But we must do them all in the utter realization that only God can cause love to grow within our souls. And we know that it is His will that we grow in love.

As we do our part, we can count on God to perform His, not because our working obligates Him to work but because He is a gracious and loving God and wants us to become gracious and loving children of His.

EXERCISES FOR PRACTICE AND DISCUSSION

1. Read Mark 15:16-37 and set aside some time to think about the love Christ showed in laying down His life for you. You might find it helpful to close your eyes and imagine the scene at the cross. Sometimes it's useful to picture just one object in the scene, such as the nails or the crown of thorns, and expand your picture from there. The point here is to become more vividly aware that Jesus actually did this on your behalf. Give it five or ten minutes. What strikes you?

2. What opportunities do you have to give of yourself to others, even at considerable cost?

3. What hinders you from loving? For example, perhaps pre-occupation with personal concerns keeps you from caring about others. Or your desire to spend your money on your own needs keeps you from being generous toward the poor. Or maybe you've been hurt and are unwilling to take risks in relationships. Pray about the obstacles that limit your love.

4. Whom do you need to forgive? If you find this person hard to forgive, you might meditate on 1 John 4:7-11. Ask God to help you forgive as He has forgiven you. Ask God to help you trust that His justice toward this person has been satisfied, even if you don't have the justice you'd like to see.

5. Pray through 1 Corinthians 13:1-7 as well as the list of loving motivations on pages 62–63. What motivates you to love? What motivations do you need to grow in? Consider committing verses 4-7 to memory.

CHAPTER FIVE

Joy

For the kingdom of God is not a matter of eating and drinking, but of righteousness, peace and joy in the Holy Spirit.

ROMANS 14:17

For a number of years, the virtue of joy was not very evident in my life nor very high in my value system. With regard to Romans 14:17, I considered myself a man of peace, and I felt I was seeking after the ethical righteousness that is referred to in that passage. But I really hadn't given much thought to the importance God places on the fruit of joy in our lives.

Then one day as I was reading through Romans 14, I realized that God was not satisfied with only righteousness and peace in our lives. Paul tells us very plainly that the kingdom of God is a matter of not only righteousness and peace but also *joy.* Furthermore, I learned from verse 18 that without joy, my life was really not very pleasing to God.

The fact is, only Christians have a reason to be joyful, but it is also a fact that every Christian *should* be joyful.

True Christian joy is both a privilege and a duty. Jesus said, "I have come that they [His sheep] may have life, and have it to the full" (John 10:10). He has come that our lives might be full of joy. Twice in His talk to the disciples on the evening of His betrayal, Jesus referred to the joy that He desired for them to have (see John 17:13). He has done all to make it possible for us to live joyful lives.

But we are not to sit around waiting for our circumstances to make us joyful; we are *commanded* to be joyful always (see 1 Thessalonians 5:16). We are to rejoice always (see Philippians 4:4). Paul is quite emphatic about this: "I will say it again: Rejoice!" Like the other character traits we have examined, joy is not an option available only to those whose temperament is conducive to it. God intends that every one of His children exhibit the fruit of joy.

Just being joyful is not enough, however; we should continually be growing in joy. It is a contradiction for a Christian who professes to be a child of the one and only God — who created the universe and who governs it for His glory and the good of His people — to wear a gloomy countenance. As John W. Sanderson says, "It is practical atheism, for it ignores God and his attributes."[1]

Yet if we are honest, most of us must admit that life is so often anything *but* joyful. It often seems that at best life is dull, and at worst it is filled with anxiety, conflict, and tension. What is it that blocks joy in our lives?

STUMBLING BLOCKS

One of the most common hindrances to joy is *sin in our lives*, or sinful attitudes in our hearts. Christian joy is essentially the enjoyment of God, the fruit of communion with Him. Sin obviously breaks that communion and the enjoyment of His presence. When David was confessing his sin of adultery with Bathsheba, he prayed, "Restore to me the *joy* of your salvation" (Psalm 51:12, emphasis added).

Psalm 32:3-4 vividly describes David's lack of joy as he agonized over his sin. When we are not experiencing joy, we should examine our hearts and our lives. Are we doing or have we done something that is displeasing to God that we need to confess and forsake? Or as is often the case, are we holding on to some sinful attitude, such as envy or resentment, or a critical and unforgiving spirit? The fruit of joy cannot exist when such attitudes have control of our hearts. All sin, be it in attitude or action, must be dealt with if we are to display the virtue of joy in our lives.

Another stumbling block to joy is *misplaced confidence*. Paul told the Philippian Christians to "rejoice in the Lord" (3:1). He then made it clear that the opposite of rejoicing in the Lord is to put confidence in the flesh — in our good works or religious attainment. For the believers of Paul's day, it was Jewish legalism. For us today, it might be our personal disciplines, such as a regular quiet time, a consistent Scripture memory program, or faithfulness in witnessing to non-Christians. Whatever it is, if the source of our confidence is anything other than Jesus Christ and His grace, it is a false and oft-interrupted joy. As Sanderson says, "even success in the Lord's work is a broken reed if we lean on it for security."[2]

If we are to have consistent joy, our attitude must be that expressed in the words of the old hymn:

> My hope is built on nothing less
> > than Jesus' blood and righteousness;
> I dare not trust the sweetest frame,
> > but wholly lean on Jesus' name.

In Luke's account of Jesus' sending out the seventy-two to preach, he says that they returned with joy and said, "Lord, even the demons submit to us in your name." Jesus responded,

"However, do not rejoice that the spirits submit to you, but rejoice that your names are written in heaven" (10:17-20). It appears that Jesus was not discouraging joy in the ministry but cautioning against the grounds of one's joy being in the success of a ministry. Success in ministry comes and goes, but our names are written in heaven forever. The circumstances of this life rise and fall, but the assurance of being with Christ one day never changes. It is in this fact that our joy must be grounded.

I referred earlier to the book *The Pursuit of Holiness*, which I was privileged to write many years ago. God has blessed the ministry of that book far beyond my expectations, and He has done it purely by His grace. I sometimes feel as the little boy must have who gave Jesus his five small barley loaves and two small fish, then watched in utter amazement as Jesus used them to feed five thousand people. Although I rejoice at what God has done through *The Pursuit of Holiness*, the fundamental ground for my joy should not be in a book and its ministry but in the fact that my name is written in heaven.

Perhaps you don't feel you have much to show for your life. Maybe you haven't written a book, or seen scores come to Christ through your witness, or done anything else that seems significant. But is your name written in heaven? If it is, you have as much reason to rejoice as the most well-known and "successful" Christian. Nothing you or I will ever do can possibly compare with having our names written in heaven. The most humble Christian as well as the most famous Christian stand together on that common ground.

A third area that can choke off joy in our lives is the *chastening* or *discipline* that God often administers to His children. Scripture says, "No discipline seems pleasant at the time, but painful" (Hebrews 12:11). Discipline is never a joyful experience; it is not meant to be, else it would not accomplish its intended results.

If we lose sight of its intended results, or feel we don't deserve it, discipline can lead to self-pity. John Sanderson again provides a helpful insight into the relationship between discipline and joy when he says,

> If we only knew how bad we are, we would welcome chastening because this is God's way of getting rid of sin and its habits. But chastening is resented because we cannot believe that we have done anything worthy of it.[3]

The secret of maintaining some semblance of joy in the midst of discipline is to remember that "the Lord disciplines those he loves," and that "later on, however, it [the discipline] produces a harvest of righteousness and peace for those who have been trained by it" (Hebrews 12:6,11).

Experiencing trials of faith is a fourth hindrance to joy. Trials differ from discipline in that their purpose is to exercise our faith, not deal with sin in our lives. In His infinite wisdom, God allows trials in order to develop perseverance in us and cause us to fix our hopes on the glory that is yet to be revealed.

Trials can come in many forms: nagging health problems, financial reverses, criticism and rejection, outright persecution. Whatever form the trial takes and however severe it may be, it is intended to strengthen our character. Weight lifters and other athletes have a saying: "No pain, no gain." The message is plain. Weight lifters know they have to endure the agony of lifting more than their muscles can comfortably handle if they want to increase their strength. So it is with faith. Our faith and perseverance can grow only under the pain of trial.

Frequently, our reaction to trials is like Job's. At the beginning of his testing, he reacted positively with the statement, "The LORD gave and the LORD has taken away; may the name of the LORD be praised" (1:21). But as time wore on and the trials, aggravated by the false accusations of his friends, continued, Job's faith and patience gave out. He was finally reduced to saying, "It profits a man nothing when he tries to please God" (34:9). But though Job's faith wore out, God's faithfulness did not. He stayed with Job until Job had learned the lesson of God's sovereignty, and then He gave Job twice as much as he had before.

God's faithfulness should also be of comfort to us in times of trial. "Though he brings grief, he will show compassion, so great is his unfailing love" (Lamentations 3:32).

STEPPING-STONES

Before considering any of the practical steps we can take to cultivate a joyful spirit, we must remind ourselves that joy is a fruit of the Spirit, the effect of His ministry in our hearts. Paul said in his letter to the Romans, "May the God of hope fill you with all joy and peace as you trust in him, so that you may overflow with hope by the power of the Holy Spirit" (15:13). It is by the power of the Holy Spirit that we experience the joy of salvation and are enabled to rejoice even in the midst of trials.

The Holy Spirit uses His Word to create joy in our hearts. Romans 15 contains an interesting connection between God and the Scriptures. Verse 4 of that chapter speaks of the endurance and encouragement that come from the Scriptures; verse 5 says God gives endurance and encouragement. That God gives endurance and encouragement through the Scriptures should not surprise us. God is the Source; the Scriptures are the means. The same truth applies to joy. Verse 13 speaks of the God of hope filling us with joy and peace as we trust in Him. How would we expect God to fill us with joy and hope? The reasonable answer is by means of the comfort of the Scriptures.

When I have experienced the Lord's discipline, the passage in Hebrews 12:6, "The Lord disciplines those he loves," has been a source of comfort and a means of restoring joy. When I was once experiencing what for me was a rather severe trial, Psalm 50:15 became a source of comfort: "Call upon me in the day of trouble; I will deliver you, and you will honor me." On another occasion when I thought my future looked bleak, I was enabled to rejoice in the Lord through the assurance of Jeremiah 29:11, "'I know the plans I have for you,' declares the LORD, 'plans to prosper you and not to harm you, plans to give you hope and a future.'"

These are the words the Holy Spirit will use to promote joy in our hearts. In order for Him to use the Scriptures, however, they must be in our hearts through regular exposure to and meditation upon them. This is our responsibility and is one of the practical means we must pursue to exhibit the fruit of joy.

But does the Word always minister to us in times of need? Are there not times when the Scriptures seem barren and lifeless and utterly powerless to arouse the spirit of joy in the face of difficult trials? Yes, there are those times, but we must remember that it is the Holy Spirit who comforts us and enables us to rejoice. His Word is simply His instrument. He works when and how He pleases, so we must look to Him with faith and patience to bring life to His Word and apply it to our hearts.

I well remember a time when our family was struggling through a series of financial reverses. There was one thing after another: injuries, emergency hospital care, things breaking down at home, frequent car repairs. The final straw was when the car broke down on a trip and we had to leave it for repairs at an unknown garage for four days. Assuming the worst, I lost all sense of joy in the Lord because I was focusing on circumstances rather than on Him. But sometime during those four days, the

Holy Spirit enabled me to rest on the promise of Romans 8:28: that God was in control and at work in those circumstances for my good. Romans 8:28 is a passage I had known for years, but it did not help until the Holy Spirit applied it to my heart and enabled me to believe it.

So again we see the principle set forth in chapter 1: We are both responsible and dependent. I was responsible to exhibit the fruit of joy during that time of financial reversal, but I was absolutely dependent upon the Holy Spirit for the power to do it. As we look to Him, though, let us remember that the purpose of rejoicing is not so we can feel better emotionally (though that will happen). The purpose of joy is to glorify God by demonstrating to an unbelieving world that our loving and faithful heavenly Father cares for us and provides all that we need.

Now for some specific practical aids to joy in our lives. An obvious one is, *Confess and forsake sin.* I have already referred to the lack of joy, or the strong spirit of oppression, that David experienced when he failed to deal with his sin (see Psalm 32:3-4). But as David confessed his sin, there was an interesting progression in his thoughts, starting with freedom from guilt, moving to faith in God's deliverance, to testimony to God's unfailing love, to rejoicing and singing (see verses 5-11).

God's forgiveness is always a source of amazement to me. It seems incredible that in spite of repeated sins, if we confess them, He is faithful and just to forgive them. And the continued faithfulness of God to forgive and to restore me to His fellowship is a source of joy to me. I am ready to sing just as David did.

A second specific aid to joy is, *Trust in God.* Romans 15:13 speaks of God filling us with joy and peace as we trust in Him.[4] It is God who stands behind His Word. The promises of the Bible are nothing more than God's covenant to be faithful to His people. It is His character that makes these promises valid.

I remember a friend of mine who, in the midst of a very deep trial, could find no comfort in the Scriptures. He asked God for some words of comfort, but none came. He finally concluded that though the promises of the Scriptures seemed dead to him, he could trust in the character of God. God fills us with joy as we trust in Him.

Consider that absolutely amazing statement of Romans 8:28: "In all things God works for the good of those who love him." That statement is true whether you believe it or not. Your faith or lack of it does not determine God's working. He is at work in all the circumstances of your life to bring out the good for you, even if you had never heard of Romans 8:28. His work is not dependent upon your faith. But the comfort and joy that statement is intended to give you is dependent upon your believing it, upon your trusting in Him who is at work, even though you cannot see the outcome of that work. God never explained to Job the reason for his trials. He simply brought Job to the place where Job trusted Him without an explanation.

Another aid to joy is, *Take the long-range view of life*. The Scriptures repeatedly affirm that the focal point of our joy should be our hope of the eternal inheritance that awaits us in Jesus Christ and the final revelation of His glory. Consider, for example, the following passages:

In this [hope] you greatly rejoice, though now for a little while you may have had to suffer grief in all kinds of trials. (1 Peter 1:6)

And we rejoice in the hope of the glory of God. (Romans 5:2)

> So we fix our eyes not on what is seen, but on what is unseen. For what is seen is temporary, but what is unseen is eternal. (2 Corinthians 4:18)

To take the long-range view is to rejoice because our names are written in heaven; it is to rejoice in the Lord in whom alone we have the hope of an eternal inheritance that far outweighs whatever troubles we are now experiencing. To take the long-range view is to follow the example of Jesus Himself, who "for the joy set before him endured the cross, scorning its shame, and sat down at the right hand of the throne of God" (Hebrews 12:2).

A fourth aid to joy is, *Give thanks in all circumstances* (1 Thessalonians 5:18). This refers, of course, to both pleasant and unpleasant circumstances. We are to be thankful all the time. This does not mean we are to be thankful *for* a difficult circumstance; rather, we are to give thanks *in the midst of* every circumstance, good or bad. We are to be thankful that God is working in this circumstance for our good. We are to be thankful for past deliverances from trials. We are to be thankful that in this present trial, God will not allow a greater burden than we can bear and His grace is sufficient to enable us to bear it. And as we give thanks to God, we will begin to experience once again the joy that is our heritage in Christ.

THE FRUITS OF JOY

One of the results of experiencing this joy is that God is pleased (see Romans 14:17-18). If Christ came that we might have joy (life to the full), if the Holy Spirit is at work in us to produce joy, then it is a contradiction of God's purpose for us when we are not joyful. Certainly, some people are more joyful by nature than others, but every Christian is to exhibit a balanced display of all the virtues of Christian character, regardless of personal temperament. We must look to God and apply all the means He has given us until we can rejoice in the Lord always.

A second result of joy is that we are strengthened physically, emotionally, and spiritually. Nehemiah said to the returned exiles, "Do not grieve, for the joy of the LORD is your strength" (8:10). Sanderson asks, "How much of our physical weakness, apathy and illness is probably due to a heavy spirit?"[5] I have experienced the direct relationship of physical strength to joy in my personal exercise program. When I am rejoicing in the Lord, the strength is there and the exercises go much easier. If I am discouraged, I seem to have no energy at all.

What is true in the physical or emotional realm is also true in the spiritual. I recall one morning going into our living room to begin my quiet time. Just prior to that, I had been sinning by entertaining resentful thoughts toward a Christian brother. As I started to kneel to pray, the thought came to me, *You cannot enter the presence of God with the thoughts you have been thinking.* Thinking of Hebrews 10:19-22, I said, "Lord, I acknowledge my sin, and it is true, I cannot come into Your presence in my own merit. I come in the only way I can come. I come through the blood of Jesus." As I uttered (and believed) those words, I thought, *What a wonderful thing that I, a sinner, having just indulged in the sin of resentment, can through the blood of Jesus come into the very presence of a Holy God.* Then I thought, *That's not all! Not only can I come into His presence, but I can call him Father.*

That little episode changed my whole day. It changed me from a discouraged, resentful person to a joyous and forgiven person. And the joy of God's gracious forgiveness enabled me to deal with the root of that resentment. Joy does give spiritual strength. The joy of discovering the sufficiency of God's grace enabled Paul to delight in weaknesses, in insults, in difficulties (see 2 Corinthians 12:9-10).

So the choice is ours. We can be joyless Christians, or we

can be joyful Christians. We can go through life bored, glum, and complaining, or we can rejoice in the Lord, in our names being written in heaven, in the hope of an eternal inheritance. It is both our privilege and our duty to be joyful. To be joyless is to dishonor God and to deny His love and His control over our lives. It is practical atheism. To be joyful is to experience the power of the Holy Spirit within us and to say to a watching world, "Our God reigns."

EXERCISES FOR PRACTICE AND DISCUSSION

1. On a scale of 0 to 5, how joyful are you? Why is that?

2. How are you currently up against one or more of these hindrances to joy?

   > Sin
   > Discipline from the Lord
   > Trials
   > A melancholy temperament

3. According to the Scriptures in this chapter, what reasons for joy do you have, despite temperament or circumstances?

4. Which of these reasons are deeply compelling for you? Which do you find harder to fully embrace and be moved by?

5. Choose one of these passages for meditation. What does your heart most need to hear from God and respond to?

   > Hebrews 12:1-3 (the joy awaiting you in heaven)
   >
   > Jeremiah 17:7-8 (confidence in the Lord, which is the root of firm joy)
   >
   > Psalm 32:3-5 (the joy of confessing sin and receiving God's forgiveness)

CHAPTER SIX

Peace

If it is possible, as far as it depends on you,
live at peace with everyone.

ROMANS 12:18

Untold millions of dollars are spent annually in search of peace. Every year, thousands of people seeking personal or family peace flock to professional counselors. Diplomats fly around the world pursuing peace between nations. Our court systems are jammed with cases arising from a breakdown of peace between individuals or corporations.

Christians are not exempt from this turmoil of a sinful world. We, too, experience the anxiety of disquieting circumstances and the anguish of broken relationships. But peace should be a hallmark of the godly person, first because it is a godlike trait: God is called the God of peace several times in the New Testament. He took the initiative to establish peace with rebellious men, and He is the author of personal peace as well as peace among men. Peace should be part of our character also because God has promised us His peace, because He has commanded us to let peace rule in our lives and relationships, and because peace is a fruit of the Spirit and therefore an evidence of His working in our lives.

A close look at Scripture reveals that peace is actually threefold:

- Peace with God
- Peace within ourselves
- Peace with other people

These are not three parallel but unrelated types of peace; rather, they are three different expressions of one peace — the peace that God gives, which is called the fruit of the Spirit. These different facets complement and reinforce one another, producing an overall character trait. Each aspect has unique characteristics that contribute in varying ways to the life of a man or woman of peace.

PEACE WITH GOD

The basis of our peace with God is our justification by faith in Jesus Christ. Scripture says, "Therefore, since we have been justified through faith, we have peace with God through our Lord Jesus Christ" (Romans 5:1). This is the point at which all peace begins. We cannot have peace within or peace with other people until we first have peace with God.

Prior to our salvation, because we were born in sin, our relationship with God was characterized by alienation and enmity (see Colossians 1:21). We were objects of His wrath and in a state of rebellion against Him. Even though the religious stupor in which we lived and the particular circumstances which surrounded us may have given us a false sense of peace, in reality we were "like the tossing sea, which cannot rest, whose waves cast up mire and mud," because, as God has said, "There is no peace for the wicked" (Isaiah 57:20-21).

Upon entering a personal relationship with God through

faith in Jesus Christ, however, all this changes. Instead of being opposed to us, God is now for us. Instead of leaving us to the mercy of circumstances, He promises to work in all of them for our good (see Romans 8:28). Proverbs 16:7 tells us that He even promises to make our enemies live at peace with us.

Peace with God, then, is the foundation of peace within ourselves and peace with other people. This foundation does not guarantee, of course, that these other aspects of peace occur automatically. We must pursue what makes for peace, both within and without, in dependence upon the Holy Spirit, realizing that the fruit of peace is His fruit, not ours.

PERSONAL PEACE

One of the petty offenses for which we arrest people is disturbing the peace. Even though a Christian has experienced peace *with* God, there are certain "disturbers of the peace" that keep one from experiencing the peace *of* God. Like the noisy or quarrelsome offenses against society, these disturbers are often petty in nature. The more calamitous events in our lives usually force us to turn to the Lord with all our hearts, and, in so doing, we experience His grace and peace. But the more ordinary adversities of life rob us of peace because we have a tendency to try to deal with these events ourselves. We worry, fret, and scheme over distressing circumstances, and we envy or resent other people who appear to get a better deal in life or who mistreat us in some way.

As Jesus finished talking to His disciples on the evening of His betrayal, He concluded with these words: "I have told you these things, so that in me you may have peace. In this world you will have trouble. But take heart! I have overcome the world" (John 16:33). In this assurance of peace, Jesus made two promises.

His first promise was that we will have trouble in the world. The same circumstances that rob us of our joy also rob us of our peace. The common denominator of all these circumstances is uncertainty. A loved one is ill, and the diagnosis is uncertain. Or our car breaks down while on a trip; will we have enough money to pay for repairs and perhaps extra meals and lodging? How will we get to our destination in time? Our luggage fails to arrive with us on an airline flight. Will we ever see it again? What will we do until it is returned to us? These and countless other circumstances continue to prove that Jesus was indeed correct when He promised us that we will have trouble in the world.

But the second promise that Jesus made was just as correct: He has overcome the world. Ephesians 1:22 tells us that "God placed all things under his feet and appointed him to be head over everything for the church"; that is, Jesus has been appointed head over everything *on behalf* of the church. He has power over all the universe, and He exercises it on our behalf and for our good. In Matthew 10:29-31, Jesus tells us that not even a sparrow can fall to the ground apart from the will of our Father. And even the very hairs of our head are all numbered. No detail is too small that it escapes the Father's attention. And now Jesus, in His ascended glory, exercises that same watchful care on our behalf.

So why do we worry? Because we do not believe. We are not really convinced that the same Jesus who can keep a sparrow in the air knows where our lost luggage is, or how we are going to pay that car repair bill, or how we can get to our destination on time. Or if we believe that He *can* deliver us through our difficulties, we doubt if He *will*. We let Satan sow seeds of doubt in our minds about His love and care for us.

Two passages of Scripture will prove most helpful to us in coming to Him to find peace. The first is Philippians 4:6-7: "Do not be anxious about anything, but in everything, by prayer and petition, with thanksgiving, present your requests to God. And the peace of God, which transcends all understanding, will guard your hearts and your minds in Christ Jesus." The great antidote to anxiety is to come to God in prayer. We are to pray about *everything*. Nothing is too big for Him to handle, and nothing is too small to escape His attention.

Paul also declares that we are to come to God with thanksgiving. We should thank Him for His past faithfulness in delivering us from troubles (remembrance of past mercies is a great stimulus to present faith). We should thank Him for the fact that He is in control of every single circumstance of our lives and that nothing can touch us that He does not allow. We should thank Him that in His infinite wisdom He is able to work in this circumstance for our good and that because of His love, He would not have allowed it if it were not for our good. Finally, we can thank Him that He will not allow us to be tempted (either a seduction to evil, or a trial of our faith; both ideas are included in the Word) beyond what we can bear (see 1 Corinthians 10:13).

The result promised to us when we come to God in prayer with thanksgiving is not deliverance but the peace of God. One of the reasons we don't find this peace is because all too often we will not settle for anything other than deliverance *from* the trouble. But God, through Paul, promises us peace, a peace that is unexplainable. It transcends all understanding. And, says Paul, it will guard our hearts and minds against the anxiety to which you and I are prone.

Now, if you are like me, you are probably thinking, *That all sounds very nice, and I agree with you intellectually right now. But when I am in the midst of a trying situation, I really don't experience that peace. What's wrong?*

I suggest two steps to take when in this kind of dilemma. First, examine your motives — you may want deliverance instead of peace. Are you looking for the wrong answer? Second, look to the Holy Spirit to bring you that peace. Remember, peace is the fruit of the Spirit. It is His work to produce peace within you. Your responsibility is to come in prayer, asking for the peace and looking to Him for it.

I doubt that any Christian is more vulnerable to worry and fretfulness than I am. I sympathize with others who are also prone to anxiety. I am well aware that it is only by the power of the Holy Spirit that we can experience His peace. But God tells us in His Word that His peace is available, and we must not be content until we experience it (see Philippians 4:7). We must persevere in prayer until He answers.

In addition to Philippians 4:6-7, a second passage of Scripture that can help us deal with anxiety is 1 Peter 5:7-9: "Cast all your anxiety on him because he cares for you." In the next verse, Peter tells us to be alert to the Devil, who prowls around looking for someone to devour. One of the many ways in which the Devil tries to devour us is related to the meaning of his name. The Greek word for devil means "accuser" or "slanderer." As the prince of slanderers, he accuses man before God, but he also slanders God to man. One of the thoughts that often enters our minds when we are undergoing some trial is, *If God really loved me, He would not have allowed this to happen to me* or *If God loved me, He would provide a way out of this trying situation.*

Such thoughts come from the Devil; failure to recognize this origin causes two problems. First, we assume those thoughts originate within our own hearts, so we add to our already anxious minds a sense of guilt for thinking harsh thoughts about God. Now we have both anxiety and guilt to contend with, compounding our problem. Second, we fight the wrong battle. Instead of resisting the Devil, we try to deal with our own wicked hearts. Although there are plenty of times when we do have to deal with our own wicked hearts, this is not one of them; this is a time to resist the Devil. We have a very clear command, coupled with a promise: "Resist the devil, and he will flee from you" (James 4:7).

This is the Bible's solution to a lack of peace within ourselves: Take our anxieties to God in thankful prayer, and resist the Devil when he slanders God to us. Only when we have experienced peace with God, through bringing our anxieties to Him, are we able to deal with the third aspect of peace: peace with other people. Inner conflict and turmoil often result in conflict with others, so we must achieve inner peace to effectively pursue peace with others.

PEACE WITH MEN

When Paul listed peace as one of nine traits of the fruit of the Spirit, he was probably thinking primarily of peace with other people. He had already warned the Galatians against "biting and devouring each other" (Galatians 5:15). And in his list of the acts of the sinful nature, immediately preceding his list of the fruit of the Spirit, those actions that are totally opposite to peace are predominant: hatred, discord, jealousy, fits of rage, selfish ambition, dissensions, factions, and envy. As he began to list traits of godly character that the Galatians needed to keep foremost in mind, peace with one another must have been near the top of his list.

The importance of this aspect of peace is amply evident from major references to it in the New Testament. Here are just a few:

Blessed are the peacemakers. (Matthew 5:9)

As far as it depends on you, live at peace with everyone. (Romans 12:18)

Make every effort to do what leads to peace.
(Romans 14:19)

Let the peace of Christ rule in your hearts, since as
members of one body you were called to peace.
(Colossians 3:15)

Make every effort to live in peace with all men.
(Hebrews 12:14)

Whoever would love life and see good days . . . must
seek peace and pursue it. (1 Peter 3:10-11)

Three times in these references we are exhorted to "make every effort" toward, or "pursue," peace. The Greek word used here also means "persecute," conveying the idea of intense effort or vigilance in tracking down something in order to harass and torment. In a positive sense, it means single-minded pursuit: to leave no stone unturned in our efforts; to lay ourselves out and humble ourselves, if need be, in order to achieve the goal of peace with others.

The pursuit of peace does not include an easygoing, peace-at-any-price kind of attitude; it does not include capitulating to wrong or injustice just for the sake of maintaining appearances. That kind of behavior often leads instead to strife within ourselves. The conflicts that are disturbing our peace with others must be courageously but graciously faced and dealt with. Pursuing peace does not mean running away from the causes of discord.

Let's consider some practical, biblical steps we can take to pursue peace in conflicts with other believers:

First, *We must remember that we are fellow members of the same body.* Paul says, "The body is a unit, though it is made up of many parts; and though all its parts are many, they form one body. So it is with Christ" (I Corinthians 12:12). Further on in the same chapter, he says the goal is "so that there should be no division in the body, but that its parts should have equal concern for each other" (verse 25). It is incredible that different parts of the same body could be at war among themselves! I am convinced there would be much less disharmony and conflict among believers if we constantly kept in mind that we are members of the same body.

Paul puts it even more strongly in Romans 12:5: "Each member belongs to all the others." Not only are we members of the same body, we *belong* to one another. That person with whom you have difficulty maintaining peace belongs to you, and you belong to that believer. What a contradiction to the unity of the body when there is discord among its members.

Not only must we remember that we are fellow members of one body, *We must also keep in mind that it is Christ's body of which we are members.* It is His glory — and the honor of His church — that is at stake in our relationships with one another. Few things are as dishonoring to the cause of Christ as Christians quarreling among themselves. Yet we expel people from our fellowship for adultery, while we tolerate discord between ourselves and other believers. We have failed to understand and obey the biblical imperative to "make every effort to do what leads to peace."

Third, *We must recognize that the cause of discord often lies wholly or partly with us.* We must seek a genuine spirit of humility about our own responsibility rather than entirely blaming the other person. On occasion, I have been an observer to discord between believers in which both parties wholly blamed the other for the conflict. Neither was willing to accept any responsibility for a misunderstanding. As we pursue peace, we must be prepared to face up to and acknowledge to the other party any wrong attitude, action, or words on our part.

Finally, *We must take the initiative to restore peace.* Jesus taught that it makes no difference whether you have wronged or been wronged. Either way, you are always responsible to initiate efforts toward peace (see Matthew 5:23-24; 18:15). If we are serious about intently pursuing peace, we won't be concerned about which of us is the offending party. We will have one goal: to restore peace in a godly manner. Unresolved conflict between believers is sin and must be treated as such; otherwise, it will spread throughout the body like cancer until it requires radical spiritual surgery. Far better to deal with it when it is easily contained.

There may be times, however, when you have pursued peace to no avail. The Bible recognizes that possibility (see Romans 12:18), but be sure you have done all you can to restore peace.

The "going to your brother" of Matthew 5 and Matthew 18 relates to conflict among believers; pursuing peace with unbelievers requires a somewhat different approach. Obviously, we are not members of one body. We do not share the work of the Holy Spirit in enabling us to restore peace. How, then, should we handle conflict with unbelievers?

First, *If we have offended an unbeliever, it is our responsibility to take steps to restore peace.* Sometimes this is more humbling than going to a believer to acknowledge a wrong; the unbeliever is not as apt to respond in a gracious and forgiving manner. But humbling or not, we must do this if we are to maintain a Christian testimony.

What should we do, however, when the unbeliever wrongs us? When there is no common bond, no fellowship to be restored, no mutual presence of the Holy Spirit to aid in restoration, then we tend to think in terms of revenge — if not in action, at least in our thoughts.

I believe that Romans 12:17-21 provides the answer. As we look at this passage we see that first, *We are to do everything we possibly can to maintain peace,* as far as it depends on us.

Second, *We are in no way to seek revenge.* We are not to repay evil for evil; we are to leave the matter of justice in the hands of God. So often when we have been wronged, or think we have been wronged, we imagine getting even with the other person. We don't *intend* to take revenge, but we actually do it in our minds. Such an attitude is clearly contrary to Scripture. Verse 19 says that it is God's prerogative to mete out justice; His judgment alone is always according to the truth. He alone knows all the facts and all the motives behind them.

As we are willing to leave justice to God, we have His assurance that He will repay. God is a God of infinite justice; no wrong inflicted on us ever goes unnoticed by Him. Although we may never be aware of the repayment, we do have God's promise of it.

Of course, our goal in regard to an offending unbeliever should not be a desire for revenge, either God's revenge or ours. The purpose of God's assurance of justice here is not to satisfy our own sense of justice but to remove it as a consideration from our minds. In effect, God is saying, "Don't concern yourself with justice. Leave that to Me. You concern yourself with something else: winning over the offending unbeliever." We can win him over, or at least make an effort to do so, by repaying evil with good. However we may understand the expression "heap burning coals on his head" (verse 20), it seems clear that our intent should be to win him over.

Because peace is a fruit of the Spirit, we are dependent upon the Spirit's work in our lives to produce the desire and means to pursue peace. But we are also responsible to use the means He has given us and take all practical steps to attain both peace within and peace with others.

Commit to memory such passages of Scripture as Philippians 4:6-7, 1 Peter 5:7, Romans 12:18, and any others you find especially helpful. Begin to meditate upon them and ask the Holy Spirit to bring them to your mind on the next occasion in which you especially need to follow their teaching. Remember that practicing godliness involves spiritual exercise: meditating upon and applying God's Word under the direction of our teacher, the Holy Spirit.

EXERCISES FOR PRACTICE AND DISCUSSION

1. On a scale of 0 to 5, how would you assess your . . .

   peace with God?
   peace within yourself?
   peace with others?

2. What, if anything, is currently disturbing your peace?

3. How does the Devil slander God to you? If it applies to you, complete this sentence: "If God really loved me . . . "

4. Talk to God about anything you're worried about, casting your anxieties on Him. If it's hard to focus your mind, you could write your prayer.

5. For what can you be thankful in your current circumstances?

6. Why isn't peace-at-any-price a good route to true peace with others?

7. If you have wronged someone or have been wronged by someone, what can you do to restore peace? What attitudes do you need to cultivate through prayer?

8. Choose one of these passages for meditation: Philippians 4:6-7, 1 Peter 5:7, or Romans 12:18. What is God saying to your heart?

CHAPTER SEVEN

Patience

Clothe yourselves with . . . patience. Bear with each other and
forgive whatever grievances you may have against one another.

COLOSSIANS 3:12-13

C hristian character is like a single garment woven from
threads of varying colors and shades. From a distance,
the garment appears to be a single color, but closer examination reveals that it takes a combination of different-colored
threads to produce the overall effect. The casual observer is
not overly concerned with those various threads; he notices
and appreciates the garment's overall effect. But the creator
of that cloth has to consider each thread individually, ensuring
that the right shades and colors correctly follow the pattern
of the design.

Some of the traits of godly character appear to blend together
much as different shades of thread in a garment or colors in a
rainbow. Patience, for example, closely resembles joy and peace
in its effect upon our lives. The word *patience*, as we use it in
everyday speech, actually stands for several different words in
the New Testament and is used to describe a godly reaction to
a variety of situations. These different words and usages blend
together to produce an overall quality.

The truly patient Christian must display godly patience in all of the various circumstances requiring it. Just as the designer and weaver of a beautiful cloth must consider each thread individually, so the Christian who desires to grow in patience must give attention to each facet of this quality as it applies to his or her life.

SUFFERING MISTREATMENT

One aspect of patience involves enduring abuse. The biblical response to suffering at the hands of others is called *long-suffering* in the King James Version, and that rendering perhaps best describes its meaning. This aspect of patience is the ability to suffer a long time under the mistreatment of others without growing resentful or bitter. The occasions for exercising this quality are numerous; they vary from seemingly innocent practical jokes all the way to malicious wrongs. They include ridicule, scorn, insults, and undeserved rebukes, as well as outright persecution. The Christian who is the victim of office politics or organizational power plays must react with long-suffering. The believing husband or wife who is rejected or mistreated by an unbelieving spouse needs this kind of patience.

The apostle Paul especially stresses the need for long-suffering in the life of a godly person. He mentions it in his first letter to the Corinthians, in his list of qualities that characterize love. He includes it as one of the nine traits that he calls the fruit of the Spirit in Galatians. When he describes to the Ephesians a life worthy of God's calling, he includes the trait of long-suffering. He also includes it when he gives the Colossians a list of godly qualities with which Christians should clothe themselves. He stresses it to the Thessalonians, and commends his own life to the Corinthians and to Timothy partly because patience is one of his character traits.

How can we grow in this aspect of patience that suffers long under the ill-treatment of others? First, we must consider the *justice* of God. In Peter's instructions to slaves who needed to be patient under the unjust treatment of harsh masters, he tells them to follow the example of Christ: "When they hurled their insults at him, he did not retaliate; when he suffered, he made no threats. Instead, he entrusted himself to him who judges justly" (1 Peter 2:23). Note that the opposite of retaliation is to entrust ourselves to God, who judges justly. God's justice is absolute, and, as Paul reminds us in Romans 12:19, He promises us, "I will repay."

One of the thoughts that most disturbs a suffering Christian who has not learned patience is this issue of justice. He is concerned that his tormentor will escape justice, that he will not receive the punishment he deserves. The patient Christian who suffers leaves this issue in the hands of God. He is confident that God will render justice, though he knows that this may not occur until the time of our Lord's return (see 2 Thessalonians 1:6-7). Instead of hoping and waiting for an opportunity for revenge, he prays for God's forgiveness of his tormentors, just as Jesus and the martyr Stephen prayed for their executioners (see Luke 23:34; Acts 7:60).

To develop patience in the face of mistreatment by others, we must also develop a conviction about the *faithfulness* of God to work on our behalf. Peter tells us, "Those who suffer according to God's will should commit themselves to their faithful Creator and continue to do good" (1 Peter 4:19). We should entrust ourselves to God's justice and commit ourselves to His faithfulness. God will deal not only in justice (and, we pray, in mercy) with our tormentor but also in faithfulness with us.

Joseph exemplified such a commitment to the faithfulness of God. After he had been abused by his brothers, he was able to say to them, "You intended to harm me, but God intended it for good to accomplish what is now being done, the saving of many lives" (Genesis 50:20). God can and does take the deliberately harmful acts of others and turn them into acts for good, both for us and for others. The person who is patient under mistreatment by others is the person who has developed such a confidence in the wisdom, power, and faithfulness of God that he willingly entrusts his circumstances into His hands.

RESPONDING TO PROVOCATION

The aspect of patience that is called long-suffering is also used to describe the response of the godly person to provocation by others. I use the word *provocation* to denote those actions of others that tend to arouse our anger or wrath — that cause us to lose our temper. Unlike mistreatment by others, which is often out of our control, provocation finds us in a position of power to do something about it. Someone may defy our position of authority — as a parent, teacher, or supervisor on a job — or the provoker may intentionally goad or nag us. Whatever form the provocation takes, it is often deliberate, and we are in a position to retaliate or punish swiftly and harshly.

When we exercise patience under provocation, we are emulating God Himself. In Exodus 34:6-7, God describes Himself as "slow to anger . . . forgiving wickedness, rebellion and sin." Daily, God bears with great patience the provocation of sinful, rebellious men who despise His authority and ignore or show contempt for His law. It is to these very people that Paul addresses the question, "Do you show contempt for the riches of his kindness, tolerance and patience?" (Romans 2:4). They despise not only His authority but also His patience. Yet God continues to show the *riches* of His patience to those who least deserve it.

The key to patience under provocation is to seek to develop God's own trait of being "slow to anger." James tells us to be "slow to become angry" (James 1:19). Paul says that one characteristic of love is that it is not "easily angered" (1 Corinthians 13:5).

The best way to develop this slowness to anger is to reflect frequently on the patience of God toward us. The parable of the unmerciful servant (see Matthew 18:21-35) is designed to help us recognize our own need of patience toward others by recognizing the patience of God toward us. In this parable, the unmerciful servant was deeply indebted to his master — according to the New International Version, by several million dollars. The king of the parable obviously represents God, while the deeply indebted servant represents each of us in our relationship to God as sinners. As the parable develops, the first servant is completely forgiven of his huge debt. But just after he leaves the presence of his master, he finds a fellow servant who owes him only a few dollars, and impatiently demands payment — even having the man thrown into prison.

We are like the unmerciful servant when we lose our patience under provocation. We ignore God's extreme patience with us. We discipline our children out of anger, while God disciplines us out of love. We are eager to punish the person who provokes us, while God is eager to forgive. We are eager to exercise our authority, while God is eager to exercise His love.

This kind of patience does not ignore the provocations of others; it simply seeks to respond to them in a godly manner. It enables us to control our tempers when we are provoked and to seek to deal with the person and his provocation in a way that tends to heal relationships rather than aggravate problems. It seeks the ultimate good of the other individual rather than the immediate satisfaction of our own aroused emotions.

The person whose temperament is conducive to losing his temper must especially work at patience under provocation. Rather than excusing himself by saying, "That's just the way I am," he must acknowledge his quick temper as a sinful habit before God. He should meditate extensively upon such verses as Exodus 34:6, 1 Corinthians 13:5, and James 1:19. He must also pray earnestly that God the Holy Spirit will change him inwardly. *Each time* he loses his temper, he should apologize to the person who is the object of his outburst. (This helps him develop humility and a sense of his own sinfulness before God.) Finally, he must not become discouraged when he fails. He needs to realize that his problem is as much a sinful habit as it is a result of temperament. Habits are not easily broken, and there will be failure. But, in the words of Proverbs 24:16 (TEV), "No matter how often honest people fail, they always get up again."

TOLERATING SHORTCOMINGS

It is likely that most of us have occasion to show patience toward the faults and failures of others more often than we do toward mistreatment or provocation from others. People often behave in ways that, though not usually directed against us, affect us and irritate or disappoint us. It may be the driver ahead of us who is driving too slowly, or the friend who is late for an appointment, or the neighbor who is inconsiderate. More often than not, it is the unconscious action of some family member whose irritating habit is magnified because of close daily association. The kind of patience it takes to overlook these circumstances is probably demanded of us most often within our own families or Christian fellowships.

Impatience with the shortcomings of others often has its roots in pride. John Sanderson observes, "Hardly a day passes but one hears sneering remarks about the stupidity, the awkwardness, the ineptitude of others."[1] Such remarks stem from a feeling that we are smarter or more capable than those with whom we are impatient. Even if that is actually true, Paul tells us in 1 Corinthians 4:7 that whatever abilities we possess have been given to us by God, so we have no reason to feel that we are any better than anyone else.

The patient reaction to the faults and failures of others is probably best described by the word *forbearance* as it is used in Ephesians 4:2 and Colossians 3:13 (KJV). Literally, the word can mean "to put up with" and can be used in a negative sense of grudging endurance of another's faults. That is obviously not the sense in which Paul uses the word. Rather, he uses forbearance in the sense of gracious tolerance of another's faults. Since forbearance is not a common word in the daily vocabulary of most people, the word *tolerance* is probably best used to describe this aspect of patience.

Forbearance, or tolerance, in the Scriptures is associated with love, the unity of the believers, and the forgiveness of Christ. In Ephesians 4:2-3, Paul says, "Be completely humble and gentle; be patient, *bearing with one another in love*. Make every effort to keep the unity of the Spirit through the bond of peace" (emphasis added). Peter tells us that "love covers over a multitude of sins" (1 Peter 4:8); love for the other person causes us to overlook or tolerate his shortcomings.

I recall an instance when a friend of mine forgot an appointment we had together. Rather than being peeved, I simply shrugged it off. Later I tried to determine why I had had such a tolerant reaction to his failure. I concluded it was because I deeply loved and appreciated this person, and the principle that Peter had stated — "Love covers over a multitude of sins" — was at work.

Paul says we are to bear with one another in order to preserve the "unity of the Spirit" — the unity applied by the Spirit to the body of Christ. We are to *make every effort* to maintain this unity. We are to consider the unity of the body far more important than the petty irritants or disappointments of others. Again, as in maintaining peace, Romans 12:5 is very helpful: "Each member belongs to all the others." When I am tempted to become irritated with my brother in Christ, remembering that he belongs to me and that I belong to him helps quell that budding sense of exasperation.

In Colossians 3:13, Paul equates forbearance with forgiveness: "Bear with each other and forgive whatever grievances you may have against one another." The thought of grievances or complaints used in this verse seems to connote the idea of fault-finding with petty actions rather than concern over more serious problems. Instead of letting those actions irritate us, we are to use them as an opportunity to forgive as the Lord forgave us.

The principle of forgiving as the Lord forgave us is taught in the parable of the unmerciful servant. The main point of that parable lies in the tremendous contrast between the two debts: several million dollars versus a few dollars. Jesus also makes a point of the timing of the two encounters: The unmerciful servant, fresh from the forgiving presence of his master, turns around and harshly demands immediate payment from his debtor.

How well this parable depicts us when we are impatient with others! Every day, God patiently bears with us, and every day, we are tempted to become impatient with our friends, neighbors, and loved ones. And our faults and failures before God are so much more serious than the petty actions of others that tend to irritate us! God calls us to graciously bear with the weaknesses of others, tolerating them and forgiving them even as He has forgiven us.

Such scriptural forbearance does not forbid correcting another's faults or confronting someone about an irritating habit. Rather, Jesus teaches us that such correction should be done with the right attitude. We are not to seek to remove the speck of sawdust — that irritating habit or fault — from our brother's eye until we have first removed the plank from our own eye. The plank in our eye can be any wrong attitude toward our brother that is a reaction to his fault or weakness. It may be irritation, pride, or a critical or disdainful attitude. Whatever our wrong attitude may be, we must first deal with it, making sure our desire to correct or confront is not from a spirit of impatience but from a spirit of love and concern for the welfare of the other person.

WAITING ON GOD

Another area in which most of us need to learn patience is in the outworking of God's timetable in our lives. Perhaps we have been praying for many years for the salvation of a loved one, for the resolution of some problem we face, or for the fulfillment of some long-awaited desire. Abraham's long wait for the birth of his son, Isaac, is the classic biblical illustration of the need for patience to await God's timing. Like Abraham, many of us have attempted to speed up God's timetable or to substitute another solution, as Sarah and Abraham did with Ishmael, only to end up with sorrow instead of fulfillment.

Saul is another example of one who would not wait for the fulfillment of God's timetable, and for this he lost his kingdom. Both Abraham and Saul grew impatient because of unbelief in the faithfulness of God and an unwillingness to wait on Him. God, in His sovereign grace, gave Abraham another chance, and so he became the father of those who believe.

In contrast to Saul, David waited for the Lord to fulfill His plan for him. He consistently refused to take matters into his own hands, instead saying,

> I waited patiently for the LORD;
>   he turned to me and heard my cry.

He lifted me out of the slimy pit,
out of the mud and mire;
he set my feet on a rock
and gave me a firm place to stand. (Psalm 40:1-2)

James addresses the problem of waiting by referring first to the patience of the farmer who waits for his crop, then to the patience of the prophets who all died without seeing the fulfillment of most of their prophecies, and finally to the patience of Job, who in the end did experience the Lord's deliverance. The ultimate event for which we all wait, of course, is the Lord's coming. With the apostle John, we cry in our hearts, "Come, Lord Jesus" (Revelation 22:20).

The cure for impatience with the fulfillment of God's timetable is to believe His promises, obey His will, and leave the results to Him. So often when God's timetable stretches into years, we become discouraged and give up. I think of a desire of mine that I thought God would soon fulfill. When several years went by, I virtually gave up, but in the seventh year, God answered that prayer. I think of another answer to prayer that has occurred just recently. I had been praying for that request for so many years that when the answer finally came, I felt it was too good to be true. I think of still another God-given desire that I prayed over for some thirteen years before God answered. But when He did, the answer came in abundant measure.

Yet in spite of these long-awaited answers to prayers, I still struggle with impatience over God's timetable. I still want to give up or try to work something out on my own. I need to take to heart this admonition of the writer of Hebrews: "We do not want you to become lazy, but to imitate those who through faith and patience inherit what has been promised" (6:12). If you struggle, as I do, with the patience of waiting, that might be a good verse for you to memorize and meditate over in the months ahead.

PERSEVERING THROUGH ADVERSITY

Whereas long-suffering should be our patient reaction to *people* who mistreat or provoke us, endurance and perseverance should be our patient reaction to *circumstances* that try us. *Endurance* is the ability to stand up under adversity; *perseverance* is the ability to progress in spite of it. These two English words are translations of the same Greek word and simply represent two different views of the same quality: a godly response to adversity.

The source of adversity may be the ill-treatment of other people, as when Joseph's brothers sold him into slavery, or when Saul persecuted David, or when the Jews rejected and crucified the Lord Jesus. At other times, our trials are a result of Satan's attacks, as in Job's case. Still another source of adversity is the direct disciplinary hand of God in our lives.

Whatever the source of our adverse circumstances, the key to endurance and patience is to believe that God is ultimately in control, working out events for our good. Romans 15:4 says, "For everything that was written in the past was written to teach us, so that through endurance and the encouragement of the Scriptures we might have hope." The stories of Abraham, Jacob, Joseph, David, and Job were written so that we might have the privilege of seeing God at work, controlling their circumstances for their good and His glory. These examples should encourage us to believe that God controls our circumstances as well, even though we do not always recognize this control. For many years, it has helped me to realize that God never explained to Job why his trials had occurred. You and I are taken behind the scenes and shown the battle between God and Satan, but Job never was. He simply came to the place where he accepted whatever God allowed. Most often, we do not see the purpose of trials. But through the encouragement of the Scriptures we should hope, and through hope we should persevere.

Endurance and perseverance are frequently associated with hope in the Scriptures. In each of four instances in which Paul speaks of perseverance or endurance in Romans, it is in the context of hope. He commends the Thessalonian believers for their endurance inspired by hope. And the entire treatment of endurance and perseverance by the writer of Hebrews closely links endurance and perseverance with hope (see especially chapters 10–12). Hebrews 11, the great chapter on faith, is a part of this lengthy challenge to endurance and perseverance; it begins by defining faith as "being sure of what we hope for and certain of what we do not see."

The object of this hope, of course, is our ultimate glorification with Christ in eternity. The life we live on this earth is simply a pursuance of this hope. The author of Hebrews likens it to a distance race that must be run with perseverance. Our Christian experience is not a sprint that is soon over; it is a distance race that lasts a lifetime. It requires perseverance because the reward — the object of our hope — is in the distant future.

Endurance and perseverance are also frequently associated with suffering in the Bible. We may not like this connection, because we may shrink from the suffering, but we must come to terms with it. Endurance can be produced only under stress, whether physical or spiritual. In Romans, Paul says suffering produces perseverance. James says trials that test our faith develop perseverance. Endurance and perseverance are qualities we would all like to possess, but we are loath to go through the process that produces them. That is why God is so faithful to allow or to bring trials into our lives, even though we shrink from them.

So we see that God uses the encouragement of the Scriptures, the hope of our ultimate salvation in glory, and the trials that He either sends or allows, to produce endurance and perseverance. He also works directly in our hearts. In Romans 15:5, Paul tells us that God gives endurance and encouragement. We know from verse 4 that God uses the Scriptures but that He must also work directly, making those Scriptures meaningful and personally applicable to us. When Paul prayed that the Colossians would have great endurance and patience, he was counting on God to work directly in their hearts. We cannot explain this direct ministry in the heart of the believer, but that does not make it any less valid. The Bible constantly affirms this direct ministry of the Spirit of God (for example, see Romans 8:26-27; 2 Corinthians 1:3-4; Ephesians 3:16-19).

The fruit of patience in all its aspects — long-suffering, forbearance, endurance, and perseverance — is a fruit that is most intimately associated with our devotion to God. All character traits of godliness grow out of and have their foundation in our devotion to God, but the fruit of patience must grow out of that relationship in a particular way. Only as we fear God will we submit to the trials He sends or allows. And only as we deeply apprehend His love for us in Christ will we find the courage to bear up under them. Trials always change our relationship with God. Either they drive us to Him, or they drive us away from Him. The extent of our fear of Him and our awareness of His love for us determines in which direction we will move.

EXERCISES FOR PRACTICE AND DISCUSSION

1. How would you define biblical patience?

2. What do you need to know about God's justice and faithfulness to endure mistreatment patiently, perhaps in a current situation?

3. Do you have a temper? If so, what ideas for dealing with it do you find in this chapter?

4. Think back over the past forty-eight hours. How have you dealt with others' shortcomings? What attitudes about yourself and others would help you be more patient?

5. Are you waiting for God to do something? If so, what? Specifically, how do you think God wants you to pray and act during this time of waiting?

6. How does hope help us endure and persevere? What are we to hope for and confidently expect?

7. Choose a biblical passage from this chapter for meditation, depending on which aspect of patience you most need to cultivate. Here are some suggestions:

> Matthew 18:23-35 (a story that shows God's great patience with us)

> 1 Peter 2:23 and surrounding verses (Jesus' patience when mistreated)

> Hebrews 6:10-12 (on endurance)

CHAPTER EIGHT

Kindness and Goodness

Therefore, as we have opportunity, let us do good to all people,
especially to those who belong to the family of believers.

GALATIANS 6:10

K indness and goodness are so closely related that they are
often used interchangeably. They indicate an active desire
to recognize and meet the needs of others. Because of their close
relation, we'll look at them together in this chapter.

Kindness is a sincere desire for the happiness of others; goodness is the activ-
ity calculated to advance that happiness. Kindness is the inner disposition, created by the Holy Spirit, that causes us to be sensitive to
the needs of others, whether physical, emotional, or spiritual.
Goodness is kindness in action — words and deeds.

I tend to think of kindness in terms of our awareness of
those around us and the thoughtfulness we can express to them,
almost incidentally. Kindness may be as simple as a smile to a
store clerk, a thank-you to a waitress, an encouraging word to
an elderly person, or a word of recognition to a small child.
None of these expressions is costly in time or money. But they
do require a sincere interest in the happiness of those around
us. Apart from God's grace, most of us naturally tend to be
concerned about *our* responsibilities, *our* problems, *our* plans.

But the person who has grown in the grace of kindness has expanded his thinking outside of himself and his interests and has developed a genuine interest in the happiness and well-being of those around him.

Goodness, on the other hand, involves deliberate deeds that are helpful to others. Although the Bible uses the word *good* to refer to what is upright, honorable, and noble about our ethical or moral character, it also uses it to describe actions that are not only good in themselves but also beneficial to others.

George W. Bethune well observes,

> The best practical definition of goodness is given in the life and character of Jesus Christ: 'Jesus of Nazareth, who went about doing good.' [Acts 10:38] So far as we resemble Jesus, in his devotion to the welfare of men, do we possess the grace of goodness.[1]

Do we aspire to be Christlike? Then we must be continually sensitive to how we might meet the needs of those around us.

GOD'S UNFAILING KINDNESS

We need to constantly keep in mind that our goal of fruitfulness is to grow in both our devotion to God and our likeness to Him in character and conduct. The New Testament has much to say about the kindness of God. The first mention is in Luke 6:35. Jesus says that God "is kind to the ungrateful and wicked." Next we find that God's kindness leads sinners toward repentance (see Romans 2:4). In Ephesians 2:7, in the context of our utter lostness and sin, Paul speaks of the incomparable riches of God's grace, expressed in His kindness to us in Christ Jesus. He draws a similar contrast in Titus 3:4. After describing our lost condition, he declares, "But when the kindness and love of

God our Savior appeared, he saved us." It seems the Bible goes out of its way to portray the kindness of God in stark contrast to man's total undeservedness.

What lesson can we draw from these accounts of the kindness of God? He is kind to all men — the ungrateful, the wicked, the utterly lost and hopeless, the rebellious — without distinction. If we are to become godlike, we, too, must be kind to all men.

Our natural inclination is to show kindness to only those for whom we have some natural affinity: family, friends, likable neighbors. But God shows kindness to those who are most despicable: the ungrateful and wicked. Have you ever tried to be kind to someone who was ungrateful? Unless God's grace was working in your heart in a significant way, your reaction to the ingratitude may well have been, "I'll never do anything for that person again!" But God doesn't turn His back on the ungrateful, and so Jesus says to us, "Love your enemies, do good to them, and lend to them without expecting to get anything back" (Luke 6:35).

We need to develop a kind disposition, to be sensitive to others and truly desire their happiness. But sensitivity alone is not enough: The grace of goodness impels us to take action to meet those needs.

CREATED TO DO GOOD

Most of us are familiar with Ephesians 2:8-9, which teaches that salvation is by grace, through faith, and not by works. But we should be just as familiar with the next verse: "For we are God's workmanship, created in Christ Jesus to do good works, which God prepared in advance for us to do." This is an amazing statement. Not only are we created in Christ Jesus, born anew for the purpose of doing good works, we are created to do good works that God *prepared in advance for us to do.* Before we came to know Christ — and, according to Psalm 139:16, before we were even born — God prepared certain good works for us to do.

The English Standard Version provides a more literal translation of verse 10: "We are his workmanship, created in Christ Jesus for good works, which God prepared beforehand, that we should walk in them." The word *walk* suggests our common, everyday experience, not the unusual and heroic. We all have a tendency to rise to the special occasions of our lives, but God has created us to do our good works in the midst of the humdrum of daily living. Bethune quotes an earlier writer as saying, "Much of the happiness of the world depends upon what are termed little things; and it is rare that God honors us with heroic and famous distinctions in doing good."[2]

In 1 Timothy 5:9-10, Paul aptly illustrates the ordinariness of most good deeds. He says that in order for a widow to qualify for church assistance, she must be "well known for her *good deeds*, such as bringing up children, showing hospitality, washing the feet of the saints, helping those in trouble and devoting herself to all kinds of *good deeds*" (emphasis added). None of these items on Paul's list is especially exciting or glamorous. They are simply opportunities to do good in the course of daily living. Although this particular passage applies specifically to women, the principle applies equally to men. Most of our opportunities for good deeds will arise out of the course of our daily lives. The challenge to us is to be alert for these opportunities and see them not as interruptions or inconveniences but as occasions for doing the good works God has planned for us.

DOING GOOD AT WORK

Perhaps one of the most obvious areas in which God has prepared good works for us to do is our life's calling or vocation.

The good works God has prepared for us individually are consistent with the abilities He has given us and the circumstances in which He has placed us. When there is something wrong with my car, and a qualified mechanic fixes it, that is a good deed, in my thinking. If he did it as a part of his calling before God and as a service to his fellowman, it is still a good deed in God's sight, even though he was paid for his work.

Most honorable vocations exist to meet the needs of people. God has ordained His world so that people with various abilities meet various needs. We should think of our vocation, therefore, not as a necessary evil to pay the bills, nor even as an opportunity to become rich, but as the primary path of our Christian walk wherein God has planned good deeds for us to do. Most of us spend half or more of our waking hours at our vocations. If we fail to find opportunities to do good works there, we are throwing away half of our lives, as far as fulfilling God's purpose for us here on earth. If we feel our particular job does not allow us to genuinely meet the needs of people, we ought to prayerfully consider a change.

But let me be very clear at this point. I am talking about meeting the *ordinary* needs of people: clothing, transportation, education, health care, and so on. I am not talking about changing jobs to go into so-called full-time Christian work. If God has called you to that, wonderful! But that is not the only arena of life in which God prepares good works for us.

Evaluate your work situation; if you are a student, consider the work you are thinking of pursuing. Does it lend itself to doing the good deeds God has planned for you? What about your attitude toward your job? Do you view the job as an opportunity to do many of the good deeds God has planned for you by meeting the needs of people, or do you view it as a necessary evil to earn the money you need? If we are to grow in the grace of goodness, we must have the right attitude about our vocation.

Women who do not work outside the home may wonder how this section on vocation applies to them. If you are in this situation, homemaking is your vocation as well as a rich arena in which to do those good deeds God has called you to do. Few things are more difficult than making a home and rearing children. The dishes, the diapers, the washing, the cooking and cleaning may at times seem insignificant and distasteful; yet few, if any, vocations render greater benefits to those they serve than godly homemaking. You also may have greater opportunity for good deeds outside the home, such as ministering to the sick and lonely, providing hospitality, preparing meals for others, or caring for someone else's children. Review 1 Timothy 5:10 to see how Paul expected homemakers to be involved in good deeds beyond their own families.

DOING GOOD AT HOME

In Galatians 6:10, Paul tells us to "do good to all people, especially to those who belong to the family of believers." Our good deeds are to be scattered upon everyone, Christian and non-Christian. We are to follow the example of our heavenly Father, who "causes his sun to rise on the evil and the good, and sends rain on the righteous and the unrighteous" (Matthew 5:45).

Nevertheless, there is in Paul's instruction a priority of responsibility: first believers, then nonbelievers. I believe we can infer from this order a similar priority involving our families. We are to do good to all people, especially members of our own families. Paul told Timothy, "If anyone does not provide for his relatives, and especially for his immediate family, he has denied the faith and is worse than an unbeliever" (1 Timothy 5:8). Good deeds should begin at home. If we are out doing good deeds for others while neglecting the needs of our spouse, parents, or children, we are not practicing the grace of goodness.

I recently heard of a course on biblical marriage in which one of the lessons is titled "Who Takes Out the Garbage?" That may be a humorous title to grab our attention, but the author is on to something. Mundane household duties are sore points in many homes, even Christian homes. But for the Christian growing in the grace of goodness, the distasteful and despised duties of the home provide the opportunity of doing good deeds for those he or she loves most.

One of the rich heritages of The Navigators, the organization I work for, is the emphasis on serving others, which our founder Dawson Trotman built into the very fabric of the work from its earliest days. As a result, Navigator discipleship training always includes serving others. But when I have had opportunity to address young people on this subject, I encourage them to begin at home. It is a lot easier to clean up after a weekend conference than to clean out Dad's garage back home. Somehow it seems more spiritual to baby-sit some other lady's children for free than to help Mom with the dishes after Sunday dinner.

Husbands, most of us have a lot of growing to do in this area of good deeds at home. There are a lot of little things we can do *in* the house, as well as *around* it, to be more sensitive in meeting our wives' needs. Who *does* take out the garbage at your house? The best teaching is by example. If we would train our children to do good deeds (and they *must* be trained — they do not learn it naturally), then we must be examples to them. I wonder how many boys growing up in Christian homes ever have the privilege of seeing their dad do the dishes or mop the kitchen floor? Let us do good to all, but especially to our own family.

DOING GOOD TO ALL PEOPLE

Good deeds in our vocations and our homes are important, but there is still a big world out there for each of us, with numerous opportunities for doing good. Thus far I have emphasized meeting the physical needs of people. But because goodness is a disposition to promote the happiness of others, it certainly directs much of its energies to the spiritual and eternal needs of others. Here again, God has prepared good works for each of us, consistent with our gifts and circumstances. We need to pray, "Lord, what will You have me to do?" and then we should *do* it.

Although we do need to observe Paul's priority in Galatians 6 for "the family of believers," let us not overlook the "all people" referred to in the same verse. Because opportunities for doing good are virtually unlimited, we must be sensitive to God's Holy Spirit as He selects opportunities for us.

One kind of behavior we must guard against is the impulsive and often superficial response to the needs of others. On this point, Bethune very wisely remarks,

> True goodness is not merely impulsive, but rational and considerate — it will therefore pause, and be at some trouble to inquire what service, and how best may it be rendered. . . . Goodness should be willing to give time, and thought, and patience, and even labor; not mere money and kind words and compassionate looks.[3]

True goodness is self-sacrificing, not only of money but also of time. Like the Macedonian Christians who gave "even beyond their ability" (2 Corinthians 8:3), the Christian who wants to do good for others will often have to give time he does not have. Often this is an act of faith just as much as giving money we think we cannot afford. We will always be too busy to help others unless we truly grasp the importance God puts on our doing good deeds for others.

One of the less obvious but more critical needs that many (shall I say most?) people have is for someone to listen to them. They don't need our advice as much as our attention. A friend of mine went through a personal tragedy. I couldn't think of anything to say, so I hesitated to contact him. Finally I called and invited him to lunch. For an hour, I sat and listened — no advice, just listened. The only time I talked was to draw him out. One thing he said stuck in my mind: "It really meant a lot to me when you called last night." We hadn't even gotten together yet. Just the phone call and the invitation to lunch encouraged him; just realizing that someone cared meant a lot to him.

I believe that most people, Christians as well as non-Christians, are so starved for the genuine interest of one other person that a little bit of concern from someone who cares goes a mighty long way. One of the most plaintive statements in the Bible is David's cry in Psalm 142:4, "No one cares for my soul" (NASB). Do you know someone who possibly feels that way? If so, you have an opportunity to do good to that person by saying, "I just want you to know I care."

True goodness is not only self-sacrificing but also untiring. It does not "become weary in doing good" (Galatians 6:9). It is one thing to do good in a few, or even in a number of, isolated instances; it is quite another to face cheerfully the prospect of doing some particular deed of goodness day in and day out for an interminable period of time, particularly if those deeds are taken for granted by the recipients. But true goodness does not look to the recipients, or even to the results, of its deeds for its reward. It looks to God alone, and, finding His smile of approval, it gains the needed strength to carry on.

Perhaps one of the most sobering statements in the Bible is found in Hebrews 12:14: "Without holiness no one will see the Lord." It is not my profession but my holiness that proves the validity of my Christian experience and my possession of eternal life. But Jesus' account of the judgment day recorded in Matthew 25 is just as sobering. There the test is good deeds: feeding the hungry, giving water to the thirsty, clothing the needy, showing hospitality to the stranger, attending to the sick, and visiting those in prison. Jesus is teaching in that passage not that doing good deeds earns our admittance to heaven but that they are necessary and vital evidences that we are bound for heaven. Bethune explains,

> And so in the judgment day, the inquiry will be made not into our opinions or professions alone, but into our deeds, as proving the correctness of our faith and the sincerity of our professions. Never can we know that we are in the right way, except we walk in the footsteps of Him, who did good in all his life and death. He came from heaven to do good on earth, that we in doing good might tread the path to heaven.[4]

Without holiness, no one will see the Lord. The essence of Matthew 25:31-46 is that without goodness, no one will see the Lord. Both of these thoughts are very sobering to the one who takes seriously the words of Scripture.

WATCHING FOR OPPORTUNITIES

One objective in studying godly character traits is to become more conscious of the vital importance of some of the perhaps lesser-known qualities. Have you ever reflected, for example, on how important good deeds are to Jesus, as He indicates in Matthew 25:31-46? What better stimulation to good deeds can we have than to meditate on that passage of Scripture from time to time? Or you might prayerfully consider the truth of Ephesians 2:10, asking God to make clear to you some of the good works that He has prepared for you to do.

Consider your gifts, your talents, your vocation, and your circumstances as a special trust from God with which to serve Him by serving others. As Peter says, "Each one should use whatever gift he has received to serve others, faithfully administering God's grace in its various forms" (1 Peter 4:10). Remember that you are responsible not for doing all the good that needs to be done in the world, but for doing what God has planned for you.

Remember also that most opportunities for doing good come across the ordinary path of our day. Don't look for the spectacular; few people ever have the opportunity to pull a victim from the wreckage of a flaming automobile. *All* of us have the opportunity to administer the kind or encouraging word — to do the little, perhaps unseen, deed that makes life more pleasant for someone else.

Accept the cost of good deeds in time, thought, and effort. But remember that opportunities for doing good are not interruptions in God's plan for us but are part of that plan. We always have time to do what God wants us to do.

Acknowledge your need of His divine grace to enlarge your soul and enable you to look beyond yourself to the concerns and needs of those around you. Then come to His throne with confidence to receive the grace you need for growing in the fruit of kindness and goodness. May it be said of each of us, as it was of Dorcas, that we are "always doing good and helping the poor" (Acts 9:36).

EXERCISES FOR PRACTICE AND DISCUSSION

1. Think back over the past twenty-four hours. How aware were you of the needs and well-being of the people around you? If you were distracted, what distracted you?

2. Why should we be kind to the ungrateful?

3. How has God been kind to you?

4. What opportunities have you had over the past couple of days to do good . . .

    in your daily work?
    at home or to your family?
    to another believer?
    to an unbeliever?

5. Do you know anyone who needs some time and attention? If so, what can you do?

6. If you often miss opportunities to do good, what hinders you?

7. Meditate on Matthew 25:31-46. What emotions does this passage raise in you? Why? How does God want you to respond to this passage?

CHAPTER NINE

Faithfulness

Many a man claims to have unfailing love,
but a faithful man who can find?

PROVERBS 20:6

Opening my concordance to the word *faithfulness*, I quickly ran my finger down the column and counted more than sixty references in the Bible to the faithfulness of God. It is not surprising that some forty of these instances occur in the book of Psalms, which recounts, more than any other book in the Bible, the struggles of the godly and their total dependence upon God's faithfulness.

Consider for a moment the absolute necessity of the faithfulness of God. We are dependent upon His faithfulness for our final salvation (see 1 Corinthians 1:8-9), for deliverance from temptation (see 1 Corinthians 10:13), for ultimate sanctification (see 1 Thessalonians 5:23), for the forgiveness of our sins (see 1 John 1:9), for deliverance through times of suffering (see 1 Peter 4:19), and for the fulfillment of our ultimate hope of eternal life (see Hebrews 10:23). We can easily see that every aspect of the Christian life rests upon the faithfulness of God, and we have the assurance that "the LORD is faithful to all his promises" (Psalm 145:13).

No wonder, then, that the psalmist says, in reflecting upon the faithfulness of God, "With my mouth I will make your faithfulness known through all generations. I will declare . . . that you established your faithfulness in heaven itself" (Psalm 89:1-2).

Even the prophet Jeremiah, in the midst of his lamentations over the judgment of God upon Judah, could still proclaim of God, "Great is your faithfulness" (Lamentations 3:23).

Actually, even a study of the sixty references to the faithfulness of God couldn't do justice to the subject: The entire Bible is a treatise on that theme. God's faithfulness appears in precept or illustration on almost every page. It is impossible to describe the acts of God without in some way touching upon His faithfulness to His own.

In our effort to become like God in our character, we must ensure that the grace of faithfulness is very high in our value system. This is not a natural virtue, as indicated by Solomon's lament, "Many a man claims to have unfailing love, but a faithful man who can find?" (Proverbs 20:6). Many people will profess faithfulness, but very few will demonstrate it. The virtue of faithfulness is often costly, and few people are willing to pay the price. But for the godly person, faithfulness is an absolutely essential quality of his character, regardless of what it might cost.

What is faithfulness? How do we practice it, and when do we exhibit it in our lives? The biblical word denotes that which is firm and can be counted upon. The dictionary defines *faithful* as "firm in adherence to promises or in observance of duty."[1] Some common synonyms are *dependable, reliable, trustworthy*, and *loyal*. The word also has the connotation of absolute honesty or integrity.

The faithful person is one who is dependable, trustworthy, and loyal; who can be depended upon in all of his relationships; and who is absolutely honest and ethical in all of his affairs. It was said of Daniel that his rivals "tried to find grounds for charges against Daniel in his conduct of government affairs, but they were unable to do so. They could find no corruption in him, because he was trustworthy [faithful] and neither corrupt nor negligent" (Daniel 6:4).

The words *corrupt* and *negligent* help us define, by contrast, what it means to be faithful in our daily affairs. The word *corrupt* is the opposite of "honest" or "ethical," and the word *negligent* is an antonym of such words as "careful," "thoughtful," and "considerate."

ABSOLUTE HONESTY

Daniel was not corrupt; he was honest, ethical, and principled. Absolute honesty in speech and in personal affairs has to be the hallmark of a faithful person. The Scriptures tell us, "The LORD detests lying lips, but he delights in men who are truthful," and "The LORD abhors dishonest scales, but accurate weights are his delight" (Proverbs 12:22; 11:1). The Lord detests lying and abhors dishonest business transactions. Not only are we commanded not to lie; we are also commanded not to deceive in any manner (see Leviticus 19:11).

Lying has been defined as "any deceit: in word, act, attitude — or silence; in deliberate exaggerations, in distortions of the truth, or in creating false impressions."[2] We lie or deceive when we pretend to be something we are not — when as students we cheat on an examination, or as taxpayers we fail to report all of our income. My friend Jerry White writes of struggling over how much to tell a prospective buyer about a used car.[3] The issue of honesty pervades every area of our lives.

On Christmas Eve, our doorbell rang, and when I answered it, I found a little four-year-old neighbor girl holding out a plate of cookies. "My mommy sent you some cookies," she said with a big smile. I thanked her and put the cookies down someplace — and promptly forgot about them, for we were just leaving for a Christmas Eve church service. A few days later as

I was walking out to my car, the little girl came down the sidewalk on her tricycle. "Mr. Bridges, how'd you like the cookies?" she asked in great anticipation. "Oh, they were fine," I said, though I had not even tasted them.

As I drove away, I began to think about what I had said. I had lied; there was no question about it. Why had I done it? Because it was expedient; it saved me embarrassment and the little girl's disappointment (though mostly I was concerned about myself, not her). Sure, it was only a social lie, of little or no consequence. But it was a lie, and God says without qualification that He detests lying.

As I thought about that incident, I began to realize that it wasn't an isolated instance. The Holy Spirit reminded me of other occasions of seemingly innocent "social lying" — of instances of exaggeration or manipulating the facts of a story just a bit. I had to face the fact that I was not quite as honest as I had considered myself to be. God taught me a valuable, though humbling, lesson through that plate of cookies.

As I have told the story of the cookies to some audiences, I have gotten a troubled reaction from a few people. Some people, sincere Christians, think I may be nit-picking, going a bit too far in this matter of absolute honesty. But consider Daniel. The record states that his enemies could find no corruption in him. It seems clear that these government officials, from their bitter jealousy and utter hostility toward Daniel, would have seized upon any inconsistency, regardless of how small or insignificant, to bring Daniel into disrepute before King Darius. But they could find none. Daniel, like Elijah, was a man with a nature just like ours (see James 5:17), but he had evidently mastered this matter of absolute integrity. We should have the same goal.

Think of the Lord Jesus. One day He asked His enemies, "Can any of you prove me guilty of sin?" (John 8:46). If Jesus had ever distorted the truth even a little bit, He could not have asked that question with such total confidence. We are called to be like Jesus — to be as absolutely honest as He was. How would Jesus have handled the little neighbor girl's question about the cookies? I don't know what He would have said. But one thing I know: He would not have lied. And neither should you or I.

Why do I go into such detail about absolute honesty in the social minutiae of life? Because this is where honesty begins. If we are careful to be honest in the little things, we will certainly be careful to be honest in the more important things of life. If we are honest about the cookies in our lives, we will certainly be honest in our business transactions, our college examinations, and even our sports competitions. As Jesus said, "He who is faithful in a very little thing is faithful also in much; and he who is unrighteous in a very little thing is unrighteous also in much" (Luke 16:10, NASB).

Our age desperately needs to reemphasize honesty in both its business transactions and its social intercourse. I recall reading an article in one of our leading business journals that quoted a number of executives as saying it was impossible to succeed in business today without compromising the truth. Probably the same attitude prevails in politics, sports, and every other aspect of our society. But we Christians are called to be salt in a putrefying society, and we cannot be such if we are not models of absolute honesty.

UTTER DEPENDABILITY

Daniel was neither corrupt nor negligent: He was reliable and dependable. People could count on him. He undoubtedly was on time for his appointments, kept his commitments, honored his word, and considered how his actions might affect others.

Few things are more vexing than relying on someone who is not dependable. Solomon observed, "As vinegar to the teeth and smoke to the eyes, so is a sluggard to those who send him"

(Proverbs 10:26). Though the term *sluggard* refers to a habitually lazy person, it is his unfaithfulness that makes him exasperating. We may be indifferent about a lazy person's habits if we do not have to rely on him. But if we are dependent upon his actions in any way, we see his slothful habits as unfaithfulness.

If our society needs to reemphasize the virtue of honesty, it certainly needs to place great importance on dependability. Dependability has taken a decided backseat to personal desire or convenience. "I'll keep that commitment if it's convenient," seems to be the attitude of our age. John Sanderson perceptively observes,

> If we probe a bit deeper, we see that "unfaithfulness" is very close to "disobedience," for the man who disobeys God has cast himself loose from the only solid support a man can have, and his direction in life will be controlled by the shifting winds of circumstances and of his whimsical desire. . . . The man who is not controlled by God has no settled reason to keep his word or discharge his obligations.[4]

For the person who is practicing godliness, then, dependability is a duty owed not only to his fellow man but, more important, to God. Reliability is not just a social obligation; it is a spiritual obligation. God is even more concerned about our faithfulness than is the person relying on us in some particular situation.

In Psalm 15, David asks the question, "LORD, who may dwell in your sanctuary? Who may live on your holy hill?" (verse 1). There follows a list of ethical standards that a person must keep to enjoy God's fellowship. And in the middle of that list there is this standard: he "who keeps his oath even when it hurts" (verse 4). God wants us to be dependable even when it costs us. This is what distinguishes godly faithfulness from the ordinary dependability of secular society.

Consider the teenager who agrees to baby-sit for a neighbor on a given evening. Then a young man calls and invites her to the football game coming up on that same night. What is she to do? Does she just simply cancel her baby-sitting arrangement and leave the neighbor to find someone else? The godly teenager will keep her commitment even when it hurts. Or she might find a substitute agreeable to the neighbor. In either case, she feels a responsibility before God to honor her commitment and fulfill her responsibility.

Lest I appear to be singling out teenagers as especially vulnerable to the temptation to treat commitments lightly, consider the businessman who enters into an agreement only to discover that it is quite to his disadvantage. What is he to do? The non-Christian is most apt to contact his lawyer to see if there is some legal loophole through which he can get out of the contract. Unfortunately, many Christians will seek the same relief. Not so the godly businessman. He may indeed see if there is some resolution to his dilemma that is acceptable to the other party, but he will not renege on his word just because it is legally possible to do so. He will keep his word even when it hurts.

Between these two extremes of the merely inconvenient baby-sitting engagement and the financially disastrous business agreement, there are numerous instances in which all of us make commitments that from time to time may prove costly to keep. At times such as these, we especially need, by God's grace, to manifest the fruit of the Spirit that is faithfulness.

UNSWERVING LOYALTY

The faithful person is not only honest and dependable but also loyal. The issue of loyalty arises most often in connection with our friends. The word has come to have a connotation of sticking with someone through thick and thin. There is perhaps no greater description of loyalty than Solomon's words, "A friend loves at all times, and a brother is born for adversity" (Proverbs 17:17).

There is no such person as a "fair-weather friend." If a person's loyalty doesn't ensure his faithfulness to another in times of stress, then he really isn't a friend — he is simply using the other person to satisfy some of his own social needs.

King Saul's son, Jonathan, provides probably the best illustration of loyalty in the Bible. His loyal friendship with David almost cost him his life at the hands of his own father. Amazingly, Jonathan realized that his loyalty to David would, in the end, cost him the throne of Israel. Whether it be in honesty or dependability or loyalty, faithfulness is frequently a costly virtue. Only the Holy Spirit can enable us to pay that price.

There is a kind of loyalty that we must avoid, however: a so-called "blind loyalty." This kind refuses to admit the mistakes or faults of a friend, and it is actually a disservice. Proverbs tells us, "The kisses of an enemy may be profuse, but faithful are the wounds of a friend" (Proverbs 27:6). Only the truly faithful friend cares enough about you or me to undertake the often thankless task of pointing out where we are wrong. None of us enjoys being confronted with our faults or sins or mistakes, so we often make it difficult for our friends to do so. As a result, most of us are more concerned about speaking agreeableness to each other than about speaking the truth. This is *not* loyalty. Loyalty speaks the truth in faithfulness, but it also speaks it in love. Loyalty says, "I care enough about you that I will not allow you to continue unchecked in your wrong action or sinful attitude that will ultimately be harmful to you."

MEETING GOD'S REQUIREMENT

As with the other graces of Christian character, the first step in growing in faithfulness is to acknowledge the biblical standard.

Faithfulness entails absolute honesty, utter dependability, and unswerving loyalty. It is to be like Daniel: neither corrupt nor negligent. Develop convictions consistent with this standard based on the Word of God. Plan to memorize one or more verses on the topic of faithfulness, either from the references cited in this chapter, or from others that may have come to your mind.

Second, evaluate your life with the aid of the Holy Spirit and perhaps a spouse or close friend. Do you seek to be scrupulously honest? Can others depend on you even when it is costly? Will you stick by your friend when he is in difficulty, and will you confront him in love when he is wrong? Don't be satisfied with generalities. Try to think of specific instances that either affirm your faithfulness or show you where you need to grow.

Where you see a specific need for faithfulness, make that both a matter of prayer for the aid of the Holy Spirit and the object of some concrete actions on your part. Remember that your working and His working are coextensive. You cannot become a faithful person merely by trying. There is a divine dimension. But it is also true that you will not become a faithful person without trying. Jesus said to the church in Smyrna, "Be faithful, even to the point of death" (Revelation 2:10). This is something we must do, even though it is at the same time the fruit of the Spirit.

Consider the reward for faithfulness. In the parable of the talents, the master replied, "Well done, good and faithful servant! You have been faithful with a few things; I will put you in charge of many things. Come and share your master's happiness!" (Matthew 25:21). It may be argued that the faithfulness here is in relation to God rather than to one another. That is indeed true. But faithfulness to God *includes* faithfulness to one another. That is the ultimate point of each of the Scripture passages we have considered. It is God who requires that we be faithful in all of our earthly relationships. So only if we seek to grow in the grace of faithfulness toward one another will we have any hope of hearing Him say, "Well done, good and faithful servant."

EXERCISES FOR PRACTICE AND DISCUSSION

1. What sorts of situations tempt you to deceive others?

2. Do you think this chapter nitpicks about honesty? Why or why not?

3. When in the past couple of weeks have you needed to follow through on commitments and keep your word? How dependable were you?

4. How have you recently treated a friend in difficulty or a friend who did something wrong? (If you haven't been in such a situation with a friend, this is still a good opportunity to reflect on the depth of your friendships. How good a friend are you?)

5. Choose one of the following for meditation:

   Daniel 6:3-4 (Daniel's example of faithfulness)

   Proverbs 12:22 (about honesty)

   Psalm 15 (about integrity and especially keeping one's word)

CHAPTER TEN

Gentleness

The fruit of the Spirit is . . . gentleness.

GALATIANS 5:22-23

Clothe yourselves with . . . gentleness.

COLOSSIANS 3:12

We pray for patience, we pray for love, we pray for purity and self-control. But who of us ever prays for the grace of gentleness? Writing in the year 1839, George Bethune said, "Perhaps no grace is less prayed for, or less cultivated than gentleness. Indeed it is considered rather as belonging to natural disposition or external manners, than as a Christian virtue; and seldom do we reflect that not to be gentle is sin."[1]

The Christian attitude toward gentleness does not seem to have changed in the more than 160 years since Bethune penned those words. I once asked a coworker in our own ministry if he was aware of anyone who was praying for or seeking to cultivate gentleness. He thought for a moment and then said no. This is not to say that the grace of gentleness is entirely absent from the Christian community, but perhaps we don't value it as highly as God values it.

Gentleness is somewhat difficult to define because it is often confused with meekness, which is another Christian virtue that we should pursue. Billy Graham defines gentleness as "mildness in dealing with others. . . . [I]t displays a sensitive regard for others and is careful never to be unfeeling for the rights of others."[2] Gentleness is an active trait, describing the manner in which we should treat others. Meekness is a passive trait, describing the proper Christian response when others mistreat us.

Gentleness is illustrated by the way we would handle a carton of exquisite crystal glasses; it is the recognition that the human personality is valuable but fragile and must be handled with care.

Both gentleness and meekness are born of power, not weakness. There is a pseudo-gentleness that is timidity, and there is a pseudo-meekness that is cowardly. But a Christian is to be gentle and meek because those are godlike virtues. Isaiah 40 is a chapter that describes both the power and the tenderness of God:

> See, the Sovereign LORD comes with power. (verse 10)

> Surely the nations are like a drop in a bucket;
>   they are regarded as dust on the scales;
>   he weighs the islands as though they were fine
>   dust. (verse 15)

> "To whom will you compare me?
>   Or who is my equal?" says the Holy One.
> Lift your eyes and look to the heavens:
>   Who created all these?
> He who brings out the starry host one by one,
>   and calls them each by name.
> Because of his great power and mighty strength,
>   not one of them is missing. (verses 25-26)

Tucked in the middle of this description of God's power are these words:

> He tends his flock like a shepherd:
>> He gathers the lambs in his arms
>> and carries them close to his heart;
>> he gently leads those that have young. (verse 11)

The same passage that stresses the infiniteness of God's power also beautifully portrays His gentleness. What better illustrates gentleness than a shepherd carrying his lambs close to his heart? Yet the Holy Spirit uses this word picture, framed with illustrations of sovereign power, to describe God. Therefore, we should never be afraid that the gentleness of the Spirit means weakness of character. It takes strength, God's strength, to be truly gentle.

An interesting and enlightening variation between translations of a phrase in Psalm 18:35 helps define true gentleness. The English Standard Version and the King James Version translate David's declaration, "Your [Thy] gentleness makes me great." The New International Version renders it, "You *stoop down* to make me great" (emphasis added). Gentleness is stooping down to help someone. God continually stoops down to help us, and He wants us to do the same: to be sensitive to the rights and feelings of others.

THE GENTLENESS OF CHRIST

Paul appealed to the Corinthian Christians "by the meekness and gentleness of Christ" (2 Corinthians 10:1). How does the New Testament describe the gentleness of Christ?

A familiar passage provides a picture of Christ's gentleness:

"Come to me, all you who are weary and burdened, and I will give you rest. Take my yoke upon you and learn from me, for I am gentle and humble in heart, and you will find rest for your souls. For my yoke is easy and my burden is light." (Matthew 11:28-30)

William Hendriksen says that the Syriac New Testament translates the word *gentle* as "restful"; accordingly, Jesus' expression is, "Come to me . . . and I will *rest* you . . . for I am *restful* . . . and you shall find *rest* for yourselves."[3] Christ's whole demeanor was such that people were often restful in His presence. This effect is another outworking of the grace of gentleness. People are at rest, or at ease, around the Christian who is truly gentle.

Matthew 12:20 gives us another picture of the gentleness with which Christ treats us: "A bruised reed he will not break, and a smoldering wick he will not snuff out, till he leads justice to victory." The bruised reed and the smoldering wick refer to people who are hurting, spiritually weak, or of little faith. Jesus deals gently with such people. He does not condemn them for their weakness; He does not come down with a "heavy hand"; rather, He deals with them gently until their true need is exposed and they are open to Him for help. How beautifully His encounter with the Samaritan woman illustrates His gentleness. Firmly, yet gently, Jesus continued to probe her need until she recognized it herself and turned to Him to meet it.

In the very act of his appeal to the Corinthians by "the meekness and gentleness of Christ" (2 Corinthians 10:1), Paul illustrated that gentleness for us. We could paraphrase his remarks as, "Acting as Christ would act in this situation, I appeal to you. I do not demand, I do not insist, but I *appeal* to you." Paul could have berated the Corinthians for allowing into their fellowship those who sought to undermine his apostolic authority, but he didn't; instead, he chose to exercise the Spirit-produced fruit of gentleness.

When Paul wrote to the Philippians, "Your attitude should be the same as that of Christ Jesus" (2:5), he was specifically referring to Christ's humility, but we can apply this command to *all* of Christ's character traits. As His followers, we should cultivate the same gentleness that characterized His life.

TREATING OTHERS GENTLY

A profile of gentleness as it should appear in our lives will first include actively seeking to make others feel at ease, or "restful," in our presence. We should not be so strongly opinionated or dogmatic that others are afraid to express their opinions in our presence. Instead, we should be sensitive to others' opinions and ideas. We should also avoid displaying our commitment to Christian discipleship in such a way as to make others feel guilty, taking care not to break the bruised reed of the hurting Christian or snuff out the smoldering wick of the immature Christian.

Second, gentleness will demonstrate respect for the personal dignity of the other person. Where necessary, it will seek to change a wrong opinion or attitude by persuasion and kindness, not by domination or intimidation. It will studiously avoid coercion by threatening, either directly or indirectly (as Paul, for example, avoided it in his appeal to the Corinthians).

Gentleness will also avoid blunt speech and an abrupt manner, instead seeking to answer everyone with sensitivity and respect, ready to show consideration toward all. Gentle Christians do not feel they have the liberty to "say what I think and let the chips fall where they may." Instead they are sensitive to the reactions of others to their words, and considerate of how others may feel about what they say. When gentle Christians find it necessary to wound with words, they also seek to bind up those wounds with words of consolation and encouragement.

Gentle Christians will not feel threatened by opposition or resent those who oppose them. Instead, they will seek to gently instruct, looking to God to dissolve the opposition, just as Paul taught Timothy to do in chapter 2 of his second letter.

Finally, gentle Christians will not degrade or belittle or gossip about the brother or sister who falls into some sin. Instead they will grieve for him or her and pray for that person's repentance. If it is appropriate to become personally involved with the erring brother or sister, they will seek to restore him or her gently, as Paul instructs us in Galatians 6, aware that they too are subject to temptation.

Christians who truly seek to obey God through gentle character will actively pursue gentleness, striving to clothe themselves with it (see Colossians 3:12 and 1 Timothy 6:11). They will place this godly virtue high on their list of spiritual traits and look to God the Holy Spirit to produce this fruit in their life.

TREATING OTHERS CONSIDERATELY

There is a trait closely related to gentleness that should also characterize the godly Christian who is seeking to manifest the fruit of the Spirit in his or her life. I have chosen to call it *considerateness*, although according to the commentators, the scriptural term requires several English words to bring out the fullness of its meaning. It appears in Philippians 4:5: "Let your *gentleness* be evident to all" (emphasis added). In the New International Version it is always translated as *gentleness* or *considerateness* (see Philippians 4:5, 1 Timothy 3:3, Titus 3:2, and James 3:17). The English Standard Version also uses *gentleness* or *considerateness*, except in Philippians 4:5, where it uses the term *reasonableness*.

William Hendriksen says a number of synonyms are necessary to show the broad meaning of this word: yieldedness, reasonableness, big-heartedness, geniality, considerateness.[4]

James Adamson uses the word *humane* in his commentary on James and says it describes "the man who is fair, considerate and generous rather than rigid and exacting in his relations with others. . . . It is contrasted with 'strict justice' and is used of judges who do not press the letter of the law. . . . It is also used of people who listen to reason."[5] W. E. Vine says it is "the trait that enables us to look humanely and reasonably at the facts of a case . . . not insisting on the letter of the law."[6]

The Pharisees, rigid in their absolute adherence to tradition, perfectly demonstrated the opposite of considerateness. They were always asking, "Is it lawful?" They never asked, "Is it kind or reasonable?" Jesus was always getting into trouble with the Pharisees because He constantly broke away from their rigid traditions and, in many cases, exposed their utter absurdity.

The considerate Christian listens to reason and is fair-minded and humane. Instead of insisting on the letter of the law, he or she asks, "What is the right thing to do in this situation?" This kind of thinking should not be confused, however, with the humanistic philosophy that says, "If it feels right, do it." That philosophy is entirely self-centered and focuses on one's carnal desires. Considerateness, on the other hand, focuses on the other individual and asks, "What is best for this person?"

Paul's admonition in Philippians 4:5 provides the proper motivation for a considerate attitude. "Let your gentleness (or considerateness) be evident to all. The Lord is near." We might rephrase it, "The Lord is standing at my shoulder, waiting to see how I will handle the various relationships I have with people today. Will I be rigid and exacting in my demands of them? Or will I be gentle and considerate, seeking to understand the pressures and insecurities they face and making allowances accordingly?" We are to show consideration to all — the store clerk, the bus driver, family members, non-Christians as well as Christians.

I fear that all too often we Christians may be less humane and considerate than nonbelievers. We think we are standing on principle when in reality we may be only insisting on our opinion. How do others see us? Do we appear to be rigid, unyielding, and inflexible, or do we come across as genial, reasonable, and humane in our relationships with other people? The Pharisees of Jesus' day had encrusted God's commands with their own traditions. Let us be careful to avoid doing the same thing.

The trait of considerateness is one of the characteristics of heavenly wisdom (see James 3:17). If we want to be wise in God's eyes, we must cultivate this trait of reasonableness and geniality.

SEEKING A GENTLE SPIRIT

I suspect that of all the character traits of godliness in this study, gentleness will be the least appealing to many male readers. For some reason we seem to have difficulty believing that manliness and gentleness can be part of the same personality. Men often want to see gentleness in their mothers and wives, but not in themselves. The macho image of the non-Christian male world has a tendency to rub off, even on us. But the apostle Paul uses the example of a mother's gentleness to describe his own character. He was able to say to the Thessalonian believers, "We were gentle among you, like a mother caring for her little children" (1 Thessalonians 2:7). A friend of mine, an ex-Marine, often signs his letters, "Keep tough and tender" — tough on ourselves and tender with others. That is the spirit of gentleness.

What are some steps we can take to develop a gentle spirit? First we must decide that this is a trait we really do want to develop. We have to decide that we want to be mild and sensitive in our dealings with others, that we are willing to live without a rigid structure of black-and-white rules. We have to decide if we really want to *care* about people.

Second, we can ask those who know us best and will be honest how we come across to other people. Are we dogmatic and opinionated, blunt and abrupt? Do we seek to intimidate or dominate others by the sheer force of our personality? Do people feel ill at ease in our presence because they think we are silently judging their weaknesses and correcting their faults? If any of these traits are characteristic of us, we must face them honestly and humbly.

As we face our overall need, we should also ask the Holy Spirit to make us aware of specific situations in which we fail to act with gentleness or considerateness. It is not enough to concede in a vague sort of way that we may be lacking in this godly virtue. We need to identify specific instances in which we fall short. Only then will we be driven to pray fervently for the grace of gentleness. And, as always, we ought to memorize one or more passages of Scripture on this topic. I suggest you quickly scan back over this chapter and select at least one Scripture reference to memorize for future meditation. Then put this need on your private prayer list, and pray that God will so work in your life that by His power you will demonstrate the fruit of gentleness.

EXERCISES FOR PRACTICE AND DISCUSSION

1. To what degree do you see gentleness as weakness or timidity? How would you distinguish between gentleness and timidity?

2. On a scale of 0 to 5 (0 = this is not at all true of you, and 5 = this is strongly true of you), rate yourself on the following qualities. Then ask a friend to rate you.

- I am sensitive to other people's rights and feelings.
- People relax in my presence. They don't have to worry about being looked down on or criticized.
- I don't condemn other people for their weakness. I speak the truth gently until their true need is exposed and they are open to my help.
- I am sensitive to others' opinions and ideas.
- I don't make people feel guilty for being less serious about their faith than I am.
- I seek to change someone's wrong opinion or attitude by persuasion and kindness, not by domination or intimidation.
- I don't threaten people, either directly or indirectly.
- I avoid blunt speech and an abrupt manner.
- I talk to people with sensitivity and respect.
- I'm not threatened by opposition. I don't resent those who oppose me.
- I don't degrade or belittle or gossip about someone who falls into sin. Instead I will grieve and pray for that person.
- I am fair, considerate, and generous rather than rigid and exacting.
- I listen to reason.

3. In what ways is God gentle?

4. Why does it take strength to be gentle?

5. What aspects of gentleness would you like to develop in yourself?

6. Ask the Holy Spirit to help you cultivate gentleness. Choose one of the following for meditation:

> Isaiah 40:10-26 (God's strength and gentleness)
>
> Matthew 11:28-30 or 12:20 (Jesus' gentleness)
>
> Galatians 6:1 (dealing with others' sin)
>
> 1 Peter 3:15 (showing gentleness and respect when expressing your beliefs)

Self-Control

Like a city whose walls are broken down
is a man who lacks self-control.

PROVERBS 25:28

I n ancient times the walls of a city were its main defense;
without them the city was easy prey to its enemies. To godly
Nehemiah, a Jewish captive in the faraway city of Susa, the
news that the wall of Jerusalem was broken down signified the
ultimate destruction of his beloved city. When he heard the
news he sat down and wept.

Self-control is the believer's wall of defense against the sinful desires that wage war against his soul. Charles Bridges has
observed that the person without self-control is easy prey to
the invader:

> He yields himself to the first assault of his ungoverned
> passions, offering no resistance. . . . Having no disci-
> pline over himself, temptation becomes the occasion
> of sin, and hurries him on to fearful lengths that he
> had not contemplated. . . . Anger tends to murder.
> Unwatchfulness over lust plunges into adultery.[1]

153

Self-control is control *of* one's self. It is probably best defined as *the governing of one's desires*. D. G. Kehl describes it as "the ability to avoid excesses, to stay within reasonable bounds."[2] Bethune calls it "the healthful regulation of our desires and appetites, preventing their excess."[3] Both of these descriptions imply what we all know to be true; we have a tendency to overindulge our various appetites and consequently need to restrain them.

But self-control involves a much wider range of watchfulness than merely control of our bodily appetites and desires. We also must exercise self-control of thoughts, emotions, and speech. There is a form of self-control that says yes to what we should do as well as that which says no to what we shouldn't do. For example, I seldom *want* to study the Bible when I first begin a study. There are too many other things that are mentally much easier to do, such as reading the newspaper, a magazine, or a good Christian book. A necessary expression of self-control, then, is to set myself down at the dining room table with Bible and notebook in hand and say to myself, "Get with it!" This may not sound very spiritual, but neither does Paul's exclamation, "I beat my body and make it my slave" (1 Corinthians 9:27).

Self-control is necessary because we are at war with our own sinful desires. James describes those desires as dragging us away and enticing us into sin (see 1:14). Peter says they war against our souls (see 1 Peter 2:11). Paul speaks of them as deceitful (see Ephesians 4:22). What makes these sinful desires so dangerous is that they dwell within our own heart. External temptations would not be nearly so dangerous were it not for the fact that they find this ally of desire right within our own breast.

Self-control is an essential character trait of the godly person that enables obedience to the words of the Lord Jesus, "If anyone would come after me, he must deny himself and take up his cross daily and follow me" (Luke 9:23). It is impossible to be a follower of Jesus without giving diligent attention in our lives to the grace of self-control.

The translators of the New International Version of the Bible have used the expression *self-control* to translate two different words from the original language. The first word, which is used by Paul in his list called the fruit of the Spirit, refers primarily to moderation or temperance in the gratification of our desires and appetites. A friend of mine who is a former teacher of Greek says it has the literal meaning of "inner strength" and refers to that strength of character that enables one to control his or her passions and desires.

The second word rendered *self-control* by the New International Version translators is a word that denotes soundness of mind or sound judgment. It is rendered *sober* or *sensible* by other translations. This word conveys the idea of allowing sound judgment to control our desires and appetites, our thoughts, emotions, and actions.

We can readily see that these two ideas complement one another in the biblical meaning of self-control. Sound judgment enables us to determine what we should do and how we should respond; inner strength provides the will to do it. Both sound judgment and inner strength are thus necessary for Spirit-directed self-control.

Sound judgment is critical to the exercise of self-control. It enables the godly person not only to distinguish good from evil, but also to sort out the good and the best. Sound judgment enables us to determine the boundaries of moderation in our appetites, desires, and habits. Sound judgment helps us regulate our thoughts and keep our emotions under control.

But sound judgment alone is not enough to enable us to practice self-control. Inner strength is also essential. All too often we know very well *what* to do, but we do not do it. We allow feelings or desires to overrule our judgment. Ultimately, *Self-control is the exercise of inner strength under the direction of sound judgment that enables us to do, think, and say the things that are pleasing to God.*

Since the grace of self-control affects so many aspects of our lives, it is helpful to focus our study of it in three major areas: *body, thoughts,* and *emotions.*

HONOR GOD WITH YOUR BODY

"And the Lord God made all kinds of trees grow out of the ground — trees that were pleasing to the eye and good for food" (Genesis 2:9). God created man to enjoy sensuous pleasures; that is, things that are pleasant to our senses and bodily appetites. The trees of His creation were not only good for food, but also pleasant to the eyes. There is no doubt that God intends that we enjoy the physical things of this life that He has so graciously provided. As Paul says in 1 Timothy 6:17, "God . . . richly provides us with everything for our enjoyment."

But man in his sin has corrupted all of the natural blessings which God has given. Because our desires have been corrupted, those things which God intended for our use and enjoyment have a tendency to become our masters. Paul had to warn the Corinthian believers against this tendency when he said, "'Everything is permissible for me' — but I will not be mastered by anything" (1 Corinthians 6:12). The moderation resulting from self-control keeps permissible things from becoming masters of our bodies.

In the rather short letter in which Paul instructs Titus in his pastoral duties among the Cretan Christians, Paul frequently refers to the grace of self-control. It is a requirement for elders;

it is important for older men, younger men, older women and younger women; it is in fact to be a characteristic of all believers. Why did Paul so stress this trait of self-control? Because the Cretans were "always liars, evil brutes, lazy gluttons" (1:12). They were demonstrably in need of the grace of self-control. Someone characterized as a lazy glutton certainly needs to learn self-control of the body.

Self-control of the body should be aimed primarily at three areas of physical temptation: gluttony (in both food and drink), laziness, and sexual immorality or impurity. Although drunkenness is a widespread sin in the non-Christian culture of today, I do not detect that it is a major problem among Christians. But gluttony surely is. Most of us have a tendency to overindulge in the food that God has so graciously provided for us. We allow the sensual part of our God-given appetite to range out of control and lead us into sin. We need to remember that even our eating and drinking is to be done to the glory of God (1 Corinthians 10:31).

What about laziness? Most of us would no doubt assent to the widespread need for self-control with respect to food and drink among Christians today. But laziness? I suspect we don't particularly think of ourselves collectively as a lazy people like those Cretan Christians. We work hard at our jobs, keep our houses painted and our lawns trimmed. Can we have a problem with laziness?

To answer that question, let's look at an incident in the life of Jesus. Mark records that "Very early in the morning, while it was still dark, Jesus got up, left the house and went off to a solitary place, where he prayed" (1:35). That Jesus got up to pray while it was still dark is challenging enough. But note what had happened the night before. Mark tells us that on the previous evening after sunset the people brought to Jesus all the sick and demon-possessed to be healed; the whole town, in fact, gathered at the door (verses 32-34). Jesus was probably quite weary at the end of that evening.

Now, you and I, under those circumstances, would have tended to sleep in the following morning, feeling that after such a full evening of ministry we deserved a rest and a little pampering. But not Jesus. He knew the importance of getting that time of fellowship with His Father, and He disciplined His physical body in order to do it.

I suspect that the number of Christians who have a consistent, productive time of fellowship with God each day is a very small minority. For some, such a time is nonexistent; for others, it is sporadic at best. This is because we tend to be lazy in body and undisciplined in the use of our time.

There are other Christians who have learned the self-control of getting up in the morning to have fellowship with God, but who haven't learned the self-control of caring for their bodies. Some are abusing their bodies through a constant lack of needed rest and recreation; others are allowing their bodies to become soft and flabby through no exercise at all. Both groups need to learn godly self-control of their bodies.

Sexual self-control belongs to both the body and the mind. There was a time, a generation or so ago, when we would hardly have felt it necessary to exhort Christians to exercise self-control in the area of sexual immorality. Control of impure thoughts, yes; but even the more moral segment of non-Christian society condemned the actual physical acts of immorality. This situation no longer exists. Authorities in our social and psychological areas today are telling us that premarital or extramarital sexual activity is okay as long as it is not emotionally harmful.

Many Christians, unfortunately, are falling prey to such thinking. Immorality among both single and married people is becoming a major concern in the Christian community. The need for sexual self-control among Christians has probably never been greater since the rise of the first-century Gentile church out of gross paganism.

God's standard for sexual self-control is *absolute abstinence* outside of the marriage relationship. If, as Kehl suggests, self-control is the ability to stay within reasonable bounds, then we must realize that God's boundary for sexual activity is limited strictly to marriage. As Hebrews 13:4 says, "Marriage should be honored by all, and the marriage bed kept pure, for God will judge the adulterer and all the sexually immoral." Paul's words to the Thessalonian believers also leave no room for compromise on this point: "It is God's will that you should be holy; that you should avoid sexual immorality; that each of you should learn to control his own body in a way that is holy and honorable, not in passionate lust like the heathen, who do not know God" (1 Thessalonians 4:3-5).

The Christian must exercise self-control not only in the area of sexual activity, but in the area of impure thoughts, lustful looks, and suggestive speech as well. Jesus said, "I tell you that anyone who looks at a woman lustfully has already committed adultery with her in his heart" (Matthew 5:28). A lustful look quickly becomes an impure thought. If *acts* of immorality are becoming a problem among Christians, the *thoughts* of immorality are a much greater problem. Sexual lust lies latent in the heart of every Christian. Even righteous Job found it necessary to deal decisively with this temptation; he made a covenant with his eyes not to look lustfully at a woman (see 31:1). If Job found it necessary to make this kind of commitment in the day in which he lived, how much more do we need it in today's society — where sexual lust is exploited even to advertise spark plugs!

The subject of control of our bodies, then, especially in the area of sexual purity, leads naturally to a second area of self-control: our thoughts.

TAKE CAPTIVE EVERY THOUGHT

Paul said, "We take captive every thought to make it obedient to Christ" (2 Corinthians 10:5). Although the immediate context indicates that he was referring to the thoughts of his opponents at Corinth, it still remains a worthy objective for the control of our own thoughts. Self-control of our thoughts means entertaining in our minds only those thoughts that are acceptable to God.

The best guideline for evaluating the control of our thoughts is that given by Paul in Philippians 4:8: "Finally, brothers, whatever is true, whatever is noble, whatever is right, whatever is pure, whatever is lovely, whatever is admirable — if anything is excellent or praiseworthy — think about such things." Self-control of our thoughts, then, is more than just refusing to admit sinful thoughts — such as lust, greed, envy, or selfish ambition — into our minds. Controlling our thoughts also includes focusing our minds on that which is good and pleasing to God.

Solomon warned us, "Above all else, guard your heart, for it is the wellspring of life" (Proverbs 4:23). The meaning of the Hebrew word for "heart" generally refers to our entire conscious person — understanding, emotions, conscience, and will; the warning is particularly applicable, however, to our thought life. It is in our thought life that our emotions and actions begin, and that sinful desires plant their roots and entice us into sin.

Our minds are mental greenhouses where unlawful thoughts, once planted, are nurtured and watered before being transplanted into the real world of unlawful actions. People seldom fall suddenly into gluttony or immorality. These actions are savored in the mind long before they are enjoyed in reality. The thought life, then, is our first line of defense in the battle of self-control.

The gates to our thought lives are primarily our eyes and our ears. What we see or read or hear largely determines what we think. Memory, of course, also plays a big part in what we think, but our memories only store and feed back what originally comes into our minds through our eyes and ears. Guarding our hearts begins with guarding our eyes and ears. We must not allow what panders to sexual lust, greed (called materialism in our present society), envy, and selfish ambition to enter our minds. We should avoid television programs, Internet sites, magazine or newspaper articles, advertisements, and conversations that arouse such thoughts. We should not only avoid them, but, to use Paul's words to Timothy, "flee from all this" (1 Timothy 6:11). It is well worth noting that in both of his letters to Timothy, Paul felt it prudent to warn Timothy to *flee* temptation. Although Timothy was a godly leader, he was not exempt from the necessity of exercising self-control.

Solomon said to *guard*; Paul said to *flee*. Both verbs convey a much stronger reaction to temptation than most Christians practice. Instead of guarding the gates of our minds, we actually open them to the flood of ungodly material coming to us through television, the Web, video games, newspapers and magazines, and the world's conversations that often surround us. Instead of fleeing from temptations, we too often indulge them in our thoughts.

We allow in our minds what we would not allow in our actions, because other people cannot see our thoughts. But God sees them. David said, "You perceive my thoughts from afar," and "Before a word is on my tongue you know it completely, O LORD" (Psalm 139:2,4). The Christian who fears God, controls his thoughts — not because of what other people think, but because of what God thinks. He prays, "May the words of my mouth and the meditation of my heart be pleasing in *your* sight, O LORD, my Rock and my Redeemer" (Psalm 19:14, emphasis added).

Television, the Internet, videos, and print media are not the only culprits in leading our thoughts astray. Paul's checklist for controlled thoughts in Philippians 4:8 includes such requirements as "true" and "noble" as well as "pure." A Christian may not be particularly bothered with impure thoughts, but may be tempted to entertain those that are not true or noble. Listening to such things as gossip, slander, or criticism about others needs to be rejected just as strongly as the tendency to pass them over our tongues.

It is impossible to listen in a condoning manner to gossip or criticism about someone else and then think only thoughts that are true and noble about that person. And if we guard our thoughts we will more easily guard our tongues, for Jesus said, "For out of the overflow of the heart the mouth speaks" (Matthew 12:34).

CURBING OUR EMOTIONS

The emotions that need to be controlled include anger and rage (the so-called "hot temper"), resentment, self-pity, and bitterness. The feelings may be explosive, as in the case of an uncontrolled temper, or they may be only simmering, as in the case of self-pity. But in either case these emotions are displeasing to God and need to be included in our efforts to exercise self-control.

An uncontrolled temper is a contradiction in the life of a person who is seeking to practice godliness. Outbursts of temper are harmful not only because they release our own ungoverned, sinful passions, but more important because they wound those who are the recipients of such outbursts. In this respect temper is a unique challenge in the area of self-control.

Ungoverned thoughts and other emotions are sins within our own minds; they harm only ourselves, unless of course they lead to sinful words or actions. But an uncontrolled temper damages the self-respect of others, creates bitterness, and destroys relationships.

We are, of course, talking here about an *uncontrolled* temper. Many believers by temperament have a tendency to lash out at those who incur their displeasure in some way. But the godly person has learned to control this tendency. Solomon said, "Better a patient man than a warrior, a man who controls his temper than one who takes a city" (Proverbs 16:32). To have a temper that requires control is not a mark of ungodliness; to fail to control it is. To succeed, by God's grace, in controlling an unruly temper is to demonstrate godly self-control.

Someone has said of Proverbs 16:32, "Note what price the Holy Spirit puts on a curbed temper; it is more to be sought than a decisive victory in war." Charles Bridges has commented, "The taking of a city is child's play, compared with this wrestling. . . . That is only the battle of a day. This, the weary, unceasing conflict of a life."[4] The person who painfully struggles, often with failure, to control his temper should take to heart God's evaluation of this struggle and be willing to pay the price necessary to succeed in it.

Although not as harmful to others, other uncontrolled emotions such as resentment, bitterness, and self-pity may be more destructive to ourselves and to our relationship to God. Uncontrolled temper is soon dissipated on others. Resentment, bitterness, and self-pity build up inside our hearts and eat away at our spiritual lives like a slowly spreading cancer.

All of these sinful inner emotions have in common a focus on self. They put our disappointments, our wounded pride, or our shattered dreams on the thrones of our hearts, where they become idols to us. We nurture resentment and bitterness, and we wallow in self-pity. Intellectually we know that in all things God works for our good, that nothing can separate us from His love. But in defiance of those God-given promises, we *choose* to think about that which is dishonoring to God and destructive of our own spiritual health.

Just as the apostle Paul beat his body (figuratively speaking, of course), so we must subdue our sinful emotions. We must deal decisively with them at their first appearance in our thoughts. Keeping a tight rein on our emotions is just as necessary to godliness as keeping the appetites and desires of our bodies under control.

BREAKING THE CHAINS OF SELF-INDULGENCE

The emphasis in the struggle for self-control should be on the word *growing*. We will never fully attain self-control in all areas in this life. Furthermore, we must realize that the battle of self-control is different for each of us. One person may have no problem at all with bodily self-control, but he may struggle with thoughts of spiritual pride. Another may never be bothered with impure thoughts but may indulge his emotions in resentment or in self-pity. As we are tempted to judge others for their lack of self-control in areas where we have no problems, let us remember our own areas of struggle and be charitable in our opinions.

Sound judgment is the beginning of self-control, and the Bible is absolutely essential to its exercise. Sound judgment must be based on a thorough knowledge of God's standard, as revealed in the Scriptures, for our bodies, thoughts, and emotions. Years ago when I first began to grow as a Christian I heard the familiar saying, "God's Word will keep you from sin, or sin will keep you from God's Word." This is not simply a cliché, nor is the Bible some magical wand to wave at temptation.

It is sound judgment, growing out of reflection on the Word of God, that warns us when the enemy of sinful desire is assailing the citadel of our hearts.

Sound judgment also enables us to form an accurate estimate of our particular needs in the area of self-control. Paul's admonition, "Think of yourself with sober judgment" (Romans 12:3), is good advice, not only for assessing our spiritual gifts, but also for assessing our spiritual needs. Proverbs 27:12 says, "The prudent see danger and take refuge." Spiritual prudence requires that we know ourselves — our particular weaknesses and vulnerabilities. Only as we study both the Scriptures and ourselves will we be able to exercise sound judgment.

Next, we must face the issue of whether we are truly willing to give up enjoying the fleeting pleasures of sin in return for knowing that our lives are pleasing to God. Kehl points out, "The beginning of self-mastery is to be mastered by Christ, to yield to his lordship. 'Wouldst thou have thy flesh obey thy spirit?' Augustine asked. 'Then let thy spirit obey thy God. Thou must be governed, that thou may'st govern.'"[5] Are you willing to acknowledge Jesus Christ as Lord of your appetites and desires, of your thoughts and emotions? If self-control begins with sound judgment, it must be carried forward by surrender to the authority of Christ in every area of our lives.

Then we must realize that the battle for self-control is fought primarily within our own minds; it is a battle with our own passions, thoughts, and desires. In those areas where we have failed to curb our appetites and emotions, we seem to have invisible antennae sensitively attuned to the corresponding temptations. The proverbial "chip on his shoulder" describes the person whose antenna is constantly searching for the minor incident that he can magnify into an occasion for losing his temper. The person who habitually yields to some bodily appetite or lust is constantly alert for opportunities to indulge that carnal desire.

We must learn to say no to those passions when they first enter our minds.

Above all, we must pray for the inner strength of will necessary to curb our passions and desires. It is God who works in us to will and to act. Our own particular areas of vulnerability must be made the subject of earnest, beseeching prayer for God's grace to work in our wills. At the same time we must realize that the will is strengthened by obedience. The more we say no to sinful desires, the more we will be *able* to say no. But to experience this, we must persevere through many failures. A large part of learning self-control is breaking bad habits and replacing them with good ones. And this process always involves a certain amount of failure.

Finally, as Kehl points out, "True spiritual self-discipline holds believers in bounds but never in bonds; its effect is to enlarge, expand and liberate."[6] James describes the Word of God as "the perfect law that gives freedom" (1:25). As we grow in the grace of self-control, we will experience the liberation of those who, under the guidance and grace of the Holy Spirit, are freed from the shackles of self-indulgence and are brought into the freedom of true spiritual discipline.

Exercises for Practice and Discussion

1. When recently have you needed each of these? How did each play a role in the situation?

> Sound judgment
> Inner strength

2. In what areas of self-control are you most vulnerable?

> Gluttony
> Sexual immorality
> Laziness toward spiritual things
> Sexually impure thoughts
> Envy
> Greed
> Selfish ambition
> Resentment
> Outbursts of temper
> Self-pity
> Other:

3. Why is it often important to flee sources of temptation and guard our eyes and ears?

4. What sinful thoughts (for instance, resentful, lustful, or self-pitying) have plagued you recently?

5. How, if at all, have you opened your eyes or ears to sources that encourage such thoughts?

6. What true, good, or praiseworthy things could you think about instead?

7. How does a person go about gaining control over what he or she thinks about?

8. Meditate on Colossians 3:1-2. What are some of the "things above" that you could focus your thoughts and desires on?

CHAPTER TWELVE

Seeking a Deeper Devotion

I seek you with all my heart;
do not let me stray from your commands.

PSALM 119:10

N ow that we have examined each of the nine qualities the apostle Paul calls "the fruit of the Spirit," we must ask: What can I do to help this fruit grow? How can I experience more and more the "new nature" Christ is forming in me? In short, how can I practice "the fruitful life"? Here we must return to a theme we began in chapter 2. Increase in godlikeness is directly tied to increase in our devotion to God.

We discover immediately that we have wonderful help in this practice of devotion and fruitfulness. We have confidence from Scripture that God gives us a new heart and moves us to obey Him (see Ezekiel 36:26-27). God gives us singleness of heart and inspires us to fear Him (see Jeremiah 32:39-40), and He pours out His love into our hearts so that we begin to comprehend His love for us (see Romans 5:5). All of this is bound up in the blessings of the new birth, so we may safely say that all Christians possess, at least in embryonic form, a basic devotion to God. It is impossible to be a Christian and not have it. The work of the Holy Spirit at regeneration assures this. God has given us everything we need for life and godliness (see 2 Peter 1:3).

But though all of us as Christians possess a basic God-centeredness as an integral part of our spiritual lives, we must grow in this devotion to God. We are to train ourselves to be godly; we are to make every effort to add godliness to our faith. To grow in godliness is to grow both in our devotion to God and in our likeness to His character.

In chapter 2 we illustrated devotion to God by a triangle whose three points represent the fear of God, the love of God, and the desire for God. To grow in our devotion to God is to grow in each of these three areas. And as the triangle is equal on all three sides, so we should seek to grow equally in all of these areas; otherwise our devotion becomes unbalanced.

To seek to grow in the fear of God, for example, without also growing in our comprehension of His love can cause us to begin to view God as far-off and austere. Or to seek to grow in our awareness of the love of God without also growing in our reverence and awe of Him can cause us to view God as a permissive and indulgent heavenly Father who does not deal with our sin. This latter unbalanced view is prevalent in our society today. That is why many Christians are calling for a renewed emphasis on the biblical teaching of the fear of God.

A crucial characteristic of our growth in godly devotion, then, must be a balanced approach to all three of the essential elements of devotion: fear, love, and desire. Another crucial characteristic must be a *vital dependence upon the Holy Spirit* to bring about this growth. The principle of Christian ministry that Paul states in 1 Corinthians 3:7, "neither he who plants nor he who waters is anything, but only God, who makes things grow," is just as true as a principle of growth in godliness. We must plant and water through whatever means of grace God has given us, but only God can make godly devotion increase within our hearts.

PRAYING FOR GROWTH

We express this vital dependence on God by praying that He will cause us to grow in our devotion to Him. David prayed, "give me an undivided heart, that I may fear your name" (Psalm 86:11). Paul prayed that the Ephesian Christians might be able to grasp how wide and long and high and deep is the love of Christ (see Ephesians 3:16-19). And David prayed that he might dwell in the house of the Lord to behold His beauty and to seek Him in His temple (see Psalm 27:4). Each of these prayers is a recognition that growth in devotion to God is of Him.

If we are committed to the practice of godliness, our prayer life will reflect it. We will be regularly asking God to increase our fear of Him, to deepen our understanding of His love for us, and to heighten our desire for His fellowship. We would do well, for example, to put the three verses mentioned above, or similar passages, on our list of prayer requests and pray over them regularly.

MEDITATING ON GOD

It is evident that the Word of God plays a crucial role in our growth in godliness. A prominent part of our practice of godliness, therefore, will be our time in the Word of God. How we spend that time varies according to the method of intake. The Navigators use the five fingers of the hand as mental pegs on which to hang the five methods of intake of the Word of God — hearing, reading, studying, memorizing, and meditating. In our devotion to God, the Word helps us in the three areas — the fear of God, the love of God, and the desire for God.

Although all of the Bible should instruct us in the fear of God, I have found there are certain passages that are especially helpful to me in drawing my attention to the majesty and holiness of God — the attributes particularly suited to stimulate our hearts in the fear of God. Here are some passages I refer to frequently:

- Isaiah 6 and Revelation 4 — God's holiness
- Isaiah 40 — God's greatness
- Psalm 139 — God's omniscience and omnipresence
- Revelation 1:10-17 and Revelation 5 — the majesty of Christ.

These Scripture selections are intended only as suggestions. You may find others that are more meaningful to you. Use them. The important point is that God uses His Word to create in our hearts the sense of reverence and awe of Him that causes us to fear Him. It is futile to pray for an increase of the fear of God in our hearts without meditating on passages of Scripture that are particularly suited to stimulate that fear.

There are also specific passages that will help us grow in our awareness of God's love. I find these especially helpful: Psalm 103, Isaiah 53, Romans 5:6-11, Ephesians 2:1-10, 2 Corinthians 5:14-21, 1 Timothy 1:15-16, and 1 John 4:9-11.

In commending certain passages of Scripture to you, I cannot emphasize too strongly, however, that it is not just the bare reading, or even memorizing, of these passages that accomplishes the desired result of growth in godliness. We must meditate on them, but even that is not sufficient. The Holy Spirit must make His Word come alive to our hearts to produce the growth, so we must meditate in prayerful dependence upon Him to do His work. Neither meditation nor prayer by themselves are sufficient for growth in devotion. We must practice both.

WORSHIPING GOD

Still another essential part of our practice of devotion to God is *worship*. By worship I mean the specific act of ascribing to God the glory, majesty, honor, and worthiness which are His. Revelation 4:8-11 and 5:9-14 give us clear illustrations of the worship that goes on in heaven and should be emulated by us here on earth. I almost always begin my daily quiet time with a period of worship. Before beginning my Bible reading for the day, I take a few minutes to reflect upon one of the attributes of God or to meditate upon one of the passages about Him mentioned above, and then ascribe to Him the glory and honor due to Him because of that particular attribute.

I find it helpful to assume a kneeling position for this time of worship as a physical acknowledgment of my reverence, awe, and adoration of God. Worship is a matter of the heart, not of one's physical position; nevertheless, the Scriptures do frequently portray bowing the knee as a sign of homage and adoration. David said, "In reverence will I bow down toward your holy temple" (Psalm 5:7). The writer of Psalm 95 says, "Come, let us bow down in worship, let us kneel before the Lord our Maker" (verse 6). And we know that one day every knee shall bow before Jesus as a sign of homage to His Lordship (see Philippians 2:10).

Obviously, it is not always possible to bow before God in our times of worship. God understands this and surely allows for it. But when we can do so, I strongly recommend bowing before God, not only as a sign of reverence to Him, but also for what it does in helping us prepare our minds to worship God in a manner acceptable to Him.

In emphasizing the value of worship, I have dealt solely with the practice of private worship: that which we should do in our personal quiet time. I do not mean to ignore public, corporate worship; I simply do not feel qualified to speak on that subject. I would plead with ministers of congregations to give us more *instruction* in the nature and practice of corporate worship. I sense that many Christians go through the motions of a worship service without actually worshiping God.

FELLOWSHIP WITH GOD

All that has been said thus far about the importance of prayer, of meditating on the Word of God, and of having a specific time of worship, implies the value of a quiet time. The expression "quiet time" is used to describe a regular period each day set aside to meet with God through His Word and through prayer. One of the great privileges of a believer is to have fellowship with almighty God. We do this by listening to Him speak to us from His Word and by speaking to Him through prayer.

There are various spiritual exercises we may want to accomplish during our quiet time, such as reading through the Bible in a year and praying over certain requests. But the primary objective of our quiet time should be fellowship with God — developing a personal relationship with Him and growing in our devotion to Him.

After I have begun my quiet time with a period of worship, I next turn to the Bible. As I read a passage of Scripture (usually one or more chapters), I talk to God about what I am reading. I like to think of the quiet time as a conversation: God speaking to me through the Bible and I responding to what He says. This approach helps to make the quiet time what it is intended to be — a time of fellowship with God.

Having worshiped God and fellowshiped with Him, I then take time to go over various prayer requests I want to bring before Him that day. Following this order prepares me to pray more effectively. I have thought about who God is; therefore, I do not "rush into His presence" casually and demandingly. At the same time I am reminded of His power and love, and my faith regarding His ability and delight to answer my requests is strengthened. In this way, even my time of asking actually becomes a time of fellowship with Him.

In suggesting certain Scriptures for meditation, or certain modes of worship, or a particular practice for a quiet time, I do not want to give the impression that growing in devotion to God is merely following a suggested routine. Neither do I want to suggest that what is helpful to me ought to be followed by others, or will even be helpful to others. All I want to do is demonstrate that growth in devotion to God, although a result of His ministry in us, comes as a result of very concrete practice on our part. We are to train ourselves to be godly; and as we learned in chapter 3, training involves practice — the day-after-day exercise that enables us to become proficient.

THE ULTIMATE TEST

Thus far we have looked at specific activities that help us grow in our devotion to God — prayer, meditation on the Scriptures, worship, and the quiet time. There is still another area that is not an activity, but an attitude of life: obedience to the will of God. This is the ultimate test of our fear of God and the only true response to His love for us. God specifically states that we fear Him by keeping all His decrees and commands (see Deuteronomy 6:1-2), and Proverbs 8:13 tells us that "To fear the LORD is to hate evil." I can know if I truly fear God by determining if I have a genuine hatred of evil and an earnest desire to obey His commands.

In the days of Nehemiah, the Jewish nobles and officials were disobeying God's law by exacting usury from their countrymen. When Nehemiah confronted them he said, "What you are doing is not right. Shouldn't you walk in the fear of our God to avoid the reproach of our Gentile enemies?" (Nehemiah 5:9). He could just as well have said, "Shouldn't you *obey* God to avoid the reproach of our enemies?" Nehemiah equated walking in the fear of God with obedience to God. If we do not fear God, we will not think it worthwhile to obey His commands; but if we truly fear Him — if we hold Him in reverence and awe — we will obey Him. The measure of our obedience is an exact measure of our reverence for Him.

Similarly, as we have already seen in chapter 2, Paul affirmed that his awareness of Christ's love for him compelled him to live, not for himself, but for Him who died for us. As God begins to answer our prayer for a deeper realization of His love, one means He often uses is to enable us to see more and more of our own sinfulness. Paul was nearing the end of his life when he wrote these words: "Christ Jesus came into the world to save sinners — of whom I am the worst" (1 Timothy 1:15). We realize that our sins as Christians, though perhaps not as outwardly gross as before, are more heinous in the sight of God because they are sins against knowledge and against grace. We know better and we know His love, and yet we sin willfully. And then we go back to the cross and realize that Jesus bore even those willful sins in His body on the tree, and the realization of that infinite love compels us to deal with those very sins and to put them to death. Both the fear of God and the love of God motivate us to obedience, and that obedience proves they are authentic in our lives.

A DEEPER LONGING

As we concentrate on growing in our reverence and awe for God and in our understanding of His love for us, we will find that our desire for Him will grow. As we gaze upon His beauty we will desire to seek Him even more. And as we become progressively more aware of His redeeming love, we will want to know Him in a progressively deeper way. But we can also pray that God will deepen our desire for Him. I recall reading Philippians 3:10 a number of years ago and realizing a little bit of the depth of Paul's desire to know Christ more intimately. As I read I prayed, "O God, I cannot identify with Paul's longing, but I would like to." Over the years God has begun to answer that prayer. By His grace I know experientially to some degree Isaiah's words, "My soul yearns for you in the night; in the morning my spirit longs for you" (Isaiah 26:9). I am grateful for what God has done, but I pray I will continue to grow in this desire for Him.

In his book *Desiring God*, John Piper writes, "[God] loves us and seeks the fullness of our joy that can be found only in knowing and praising Him, the most magnificent of all Beings."[1] One of the wonderful things about God is that He is infinite in all of His glorious attributes, so never in our desire for Him will we exhaust the revelation of His person to us. The more we come to know Him, the more we will desire Him. And the more we desire Him, the more we will want to fellowship with Him and experience His presence. And the more we desire Him and His fellowship, the more we will desire to be like Him.

Paul's heartfelt cry in Philippians 3:10 vividly expresses this longing. He desires both to know Christ and to be like Him. He wants to experience both His fellowship — even the fellowship of suffering — as well as the transforming power of His resurrection life. He wants both Christ-centeredness and Christlikeness.

Wholehearted God-centeredness, or devotion to God, bears fruit in our lives — the fruit of the Spirit. Both the practice of devotion to God and the practice of a lifestyle that is pleasing to God reflect His character to other people.

Notice that a focus on the outward structure of character and conduct without taking the time to build the inward foundation of devotion to God will fail us. This eventually results in a cold morality or legalism, or even worse, self-righteousness and spiritual pride. We must develop the inner and outer aspects of godliness simultaneously.

True character is the overflow of God's love through us. Jonathan Edwards gathered all the traits of our new nature — including the nine we've looked at in this book — into the encompassing quality of *divine love*. Edwards wrote: "Charity, or divine love, is the sum of all good principles, and therefore the fountain whence proceed all amiable and excellent actions"[2]

The practice of developing our relationship with God should never be thought of as drudgery. We are seeking to grow in our devotion to the most wonderful Person in all of the universe, the infinitely glorious and loving God. Nothing can compare with the privilege of knowing Him in whose presence is fullness of joy and in whose hand there are pleasures forever (see Psalm 16:11, NASB). From this joyful relationship flows the rich harvest of our transformed character.

EXERCISES FOR PRACTICE AND DISCUSSION

1. Which do you feel you most need to grow in right now: the fear of God, awareness of the love of God, or the desire for God? Why that one even more than the others?

2. Pray based on one of these passages:

   Psalm 86:11 (the fear of God)

   Ephesians 3:16-19 (the love of God)

   Psalm 27:4 (the desire for God)

3. Read Revelation 4–5. What essential elements of worship do you observe?

4. Why is worship essential to growth in the fruit of the Spirit?

5. Spend some time worshiping God. You can read parts of Revelation 5 aloud to Him, perhaps with additional thoughts of your own. Tell Him why He is worthy of your thanks and praise.

6. What's your reaction when you think about spending daily time with God for worship, prayer, and meditating on Scripture? What obstacles do you face, and how can you overcome them?

7. What key insights and habits will you take with you from this study? What next steps do you see ahead?

Notes

Preface

1. John J. Murray, *Behind a Frowning Providence* (Carlisle, PA: Banner of Truth, 1990), 16.
2. Evan Howard, "Three Temptations of Spiritual Formation," *Christianity Today*, December 9, 2002, Vol. 46, No. 13, 46.
3. Jonathan Edwards, *Charity and Its Fruits* (Carlisle, PA: Banner of Truth, 1978), 222.
4. Sinclair B. Ferguson, *The Holy Spirit* (Downers Grove, IL: InterVarsity, 1997), 209.
5. John Owen, *The Holy Spirit* (Carlisle, PA: Banner of Truth, 1965), 476.
6. Owen, 476.
7. Warren W. Wiersbe, *Classic Sermons on the Fruit of the Spirit* (Grand Rapids, MI: Kregel, 2002), 33.

Chapter One — Taking On God's Character

1. John Owen, *The Holy Spirit* (Carlisle, PA: Banner of Truth, 1965), 564.
2. Owen, 564.
3. In my book *The Discipline of Grace* (NavPress, 1994), I list twenty-seven character traits taught and commanded by Jesus and the apostles. These could all be considered "the fruit of the Spirit." The primary Scripture references from which I compiled my list are Galatians 5:22-23; Ephesians 4:1-2,25-32; Colossians 3:12-17; 1 Timothy 6:6-11; James 3:17. The twenty-seven traits I found are compassion, considerateness, contentment, faith, faithfulness, forbearance, forgiving spirit, generosity, gentleness, godliness, goodness, honesty, humility, impartiality, joy, kindness, love,

mercy, patience, peace, perseverance, purity, righteousness, self-control, sincerity, submissiveness, and thankfulness. I undoubtedly overlooked other positive traits.

4. I believe it is the fruit of godly character and conduct that is primarily in view in this passage (see John 15:1-6). When Jesus and Paul speak of the fruit of evangelism, they speak of harvesting or gathering, as opposed to producing fruit (see John 4:36; Romans 1:13). Certainly Jesus' use of the term *fruit* in Matthew 7:15-23 relates primarily to character and conduct.

5. Frederic Louis Godet, *Commentary on John's Gospel* (Grand Rapids, MI: Kregel, 1978), 855.

6. Jac J. Müller, "The Epistles of Paul to the Philippians and to Philemon," *The New International Commentary on the New Testament* (Grand Rapids, MI: Eerdmans, 1978), 91.

7. George W. Bethune, *The Fruit of the Spirit* (Swengel, PA: Reiner, 1839), 32–34.

Chapter Two—Devotion to God

1. John Owen, *The Holy Spirit* (Carlisle, PA: Banner of Truth, 1965), 477.

2. *Vine's Expository Dictionary of New Testament Words* defines godliness as, "to be devout, denotes that piety which, characterized by a godward attitude, does that which is well-pleasing to Him" (Nashville, TN: Royal, n.d., 492). J. C. Connell defines godliness as a personal attitude to God and the actions that spring directly from it (*New Bible Dictionary*, London: Inter-Varsity Fellowship, 1962), 480.

3. William Law, *A Serious Call to a Devout and Holy Life* (Grand Rapids, MI: Sovereign Grace, 1971), 1.

4. John Murray, *Principles of Conduct* (Grand Rapids, MI: Eerdmans, 1978), 229.

5. Murray, 230.

6. See, for example, 2 Corinthians 7:1, Ephesians 5:21, Colossians 3:22, and 1 Peter 1:17. The New International Version of the Bible uses the word reverence for "fear" in some of these passages. It is, however, the same Greek word translated as "fear" in other places.

7. Murray, 229.

8. Murray, 231.

9. Albert N. Martin, cassette tape series, "The Fear of God" (Essex Fells, NJ: The Trinity Pulpit). This series consists of nine messages on the fear of God. I highly recommend it to those who wish to pursue this subject in greater detail. I am indebted to the Reverend Martin for the definition of the fear of God used in this chapter.

Chapter Three — Humility

1. Sinclair B. Ferguson, *The Holy Spirit* (Downers Grove, IL: InterVarsity, 1997), 153.

2. Norvel Geldenhuys, "Commentary on the Gospel of Luke," *The New International Commentary on the New Testament* (Grand Rapids, MI: Eerdmans, 1977), 306–307.

3. William Hendriksen comments on this passage, "What is promised here, therefore, is that our Lord, at his second coming will, in a manner consonant with his glory and majesty, 'wait on' his faithful servants!" in his "The Gospel of Luke," *New Testament Commentary* (Grand Rapids, MI: Baker, 1978), 677.

Chapter Four — Love

1. George W. Bethune, *The Fruit of the Spirit* (Swengel, PA: Reiner, 1839), 40.

2. Bethune, 41.

3. Bethune, 38.

4. W. E. Vine, *An Expository Dictionary of New Testament Words*, 693.

5. Jerry Bridges, *The Pursuit of Holiness* (Colorado Springs, CO: NavPress, 1978), 101–102.

Chapter Five — Joy

1. John W. Sanderson, *The Fruit of the Spirit* (Grand Rapids, MI: Zondervan, 1972), 72.

2. Sanderson, 65-66.

3. Sanderson, 71.

4. You may wish to go further in this topic by reading my book *Trusting God* (NavPress, 1988).

5. Sanderson, 73.

Chapter Seven — Patience

1. John W. Sanderson, *The Fruit of the Spirit* (Grand Rapids, MI: Zondervan, 1972), 90.

Chapter Eight — Kindness and Goodness

1. George W. Bethune, *The Fruit of the Spirit* (Swengel, PA: Reiner, 1839), 117.

2. Bethune, 126.

3. Bethune, 127-128.

4. Bethune, 132.

Chapter Nine — Faithfulness

1. *Merriam-Webster's Collegiate Dictionary*, Tenth Edition (Springfield, MA: Merriam-Webster, 1999).

2. As quoted in *Character of the Christian*, Book 4 of the STUDIES IN CHRISTIAN LIVING series, 1st ed. (Colorado Springs, CO: NavPress, 1964), 26.

3. Jerry White, *Honesty, Morality, and Conscience* (Colorado Springs, CO: NavPress, 1978, 1996), 53. I highly recommend this book for further study on the topic of honesty.
4. John W. Sanderson, *The Fruit of the Spirit* (Grand Rapids, MI: Zondervan, 1972), 117.

Chapter Ten—Gentleness

1. George W. Bethune, *The Fruit of the Spirit* (Swengel, PA: Reiner, 1839), 100.
2. Billy Graham, *The Holy Spirit* (Waco, TX: Word, 1978), 205–206.
3. William Hendriksen, *The Gospel of Matthew* (Grand Rapids, MI: Baker, 1973), 504.
4. William Hendriksen, *Exposition of Philippians* (Grand Rapids, MI: Baker, 1962), 193.
5. James Adamson, "The Epistle of James," *The New International Commentary on the New Testament* (Grand Rapids, MI: Eerdmans, 1976), 155.
6. W. E. Vine, *An Expository Dictionary of New Testament Words*, 474.

Chapter Eleven—Self-Control

1. Charles Bridges, *An Exposition of Proverbs* (Evansville, IN: Sovereign Grace Book Club, 1846, 1959), 483.
2. D. G. Kehl, *Control Yourself!* (Grand Rapids, MI: Zondervan, 1982), 25. This is an excellent book for those who want to pursue the subject of self-control further.
3. George W. Bethune, *The Fruit of the Spirit* (Swengel, PA: Reiner, 1839), 179.
4. Charles Bridges, 250.
5. Kehl, 79.
6. Kehl, 26.

Chapter Twelve—Seeking a Deeper Devotion

1. John Piper, *Desiring God* (Sisters, OR: Multnomah, 2003), 49.
2. Jonathan Edwards, *Charity and Its Fruits* (Carlisle, PA: Banner of Truth, 1978), 348.

Author

D r. Jerry Bridges is an author and Bible teacher. His books include *The Pursuit of Holiness*, *The Practice of Godliness*, *Trusting God*, *The Gospel for Real Life*, and *Is God Really in Control?* Jerry is on staff with The Navigators' collegiate ministry. He and his wife, Jane, live in Colorado Springs, Colorado.

CLASSICS FROM JERRY BRIDGES.

The Pursuit of Holiness
ISBN-13: 978-1-57683-932-4

Holiness should mark the life of every Christian, but holiness is often hard to understand. Learn what holiness is and how to say no to the things that hinder it.

The Discipline of Grace
ISBN-13: 978-1-57683-989-8

If you've struggled with the difference between your role and God's role in your growth as a Christian, this book and study guide is for you. Learn to rest in Christ while pursuing a life of holiness.

Transforming Grace
ISBN-13: 978-1-60006-303-9

Too many Christians misunderstand grace and try to live up to God's love. This book helps us accept and understand God's grace so we can live with the freedom of not having to measure up.

To order copies, call NavPress at 1-800-366-7788 or
log on to www.navpress.com.

Discipleship Inside Out™

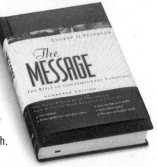